WHAT PEOPLE ARE SA

LEADINGS

Leadingship is an idea that totally resonates with these complex times! We need co-intelligence way more than we need bright individuals. We do not need to "share power" but to truly empower all players. I highly recommend this book.

Jan Bommerez, U.S.A., international speaker, business coach and author of best selling business books *Can You Teach a Caterpillar to Fly?* and *Flow and Peak Performance in Business: Seven Vital Insights for Salespeople and Entrepreneurs*.

I found the experience of this book enlivening, inspiring and exciting. It points to a way of being in the world that is not only deeply enriching and transformative, but also the master key to creating a sustainable, enlightened future for all. That's why this body of work is so important and of its time.

Dr. Mark Atkinson, U.K., founder of The Academy of Coach Training, international speaker and multi-published author.

This book really gets to the core of the essential ingredients to great leadership: authenticity and passion! Arnold strips away at all other and more superficial qualities of leadership and gets to the heart of what really matters: truth. This paradigm shifting book will surely guide anyone interested or even just curious about transforming their perspective on leadership from the inside out!

Nathalie Ménard, Canada, Principal Consultant and Business coach at Sofie Consulting Inc.

This stuff is so strong, that if you could eat or inhale it, it would probably be illegal!

Ofer Eyal, Israel, business coach and public speaker.

Leadingship

Exploring the Essence of
Leadership Dynamics

Leadingship

Exploring the Essence of
Leadership Dynamics

Arnold Timmerman

**BUSINESS
BOOKS**

Winchester, UK
Washington, USA

First published by Business Books, 2012
Business Books is an imprint of John Hunt Publishing Ltd., Laurel House, Station Approach,
Alresford, Hants, SO24 9JH, UK
office1@jhpbooks.net
www.johnhuntpublishing.com

For distributor details and how to order please visit the 'Ordering' section on our website.

Text copyright: Arnold Timmerman 2011

ISBN: 978 1 78099 861 9

A CIP catalogue record for this book is available from the British Library.

Design: Stuart Davies

Printed in the USA by Edwards Brothers Malloy

We operate a distinctive and ethical publishing philosophy in all
areas of our business, from our global network of authors to
production and worldwide distribution.

CONTENTS

If authenticity and passion were in charge...

If leading and following were non-personal...

who would you be?

Pre

For years I have known that a book would be written by me. I just didn't know when. And I kept wondering whether it would be a kid's book, a novel or an autobiography. I was on the plane to a Scandinavian leadership conference, wanting to prepare for a clinic I was asked to give, when my pen started writing: 'This book is written from direct experience, it's not written from any preconceived ideas about leadership. You will hardly find any references to clever authors, books, leaders, companies, structures, ideologies or concepts. It lacks inspiring "borrowed" leadership quotes or a magic number of leadership skills. Its aim is not to give you answers; it wants to stir up questions. This book is an open invitation to anyone who has experienced how the old paradigm of leadership is past its sell-by date – which in all honesty could be everyone! This book is an instigator for self-inquiry, an exploration of how authentic and passionate expression of ourselves can truly inspire others.'

Surprise showed up, followed by a battalion of self-criticizing thoughts. Yet, all of it was immediately overshadowed by the sheer energy and excitement that came through the body only seconds after I had finished writing. It was clear from that moment: the passion for sharing its message – even though the content of it wasn't entirely clear yet - could no longer be held back. I 'had' to follow it. And because you are reading it, another unique leadership dynamic is born. Welcome to the unlimited dynamics of leading and following. Welcome to the truth of *leadingship*.

•

The word '*leadingship*' is not new. It was just new in 2009 to this

I

leadership seeker. After two decades of trying out highly recommended and researched versions of leadership, I started exploring what personal leadership qualities were already available within me. In all honesty, I was hoping to come across a unique selling point, something that would make me stand out as a leader amongst many people. Instead, this ego-driven treasure hunt led me to the experience of *leadingship* - non-personal, bigger than me, neutral, very dynamic, outrageously inspiring. This seemed to leave no space for the known vertical, rigid, hierarchical versions of any controlling or serving leadership. A horizontal, fluid dynamic of leading and following could take its place. Wow! It 'had' to be tested, it 'had' to be shared!

Even though life seemed to 'pull' me into a new and very exciting direction, I was still too much in love with some perceived comfort and security. So instead of surrendering to that pull, I found myself complying with the structures of the known. It felt safer to go with other people's ideas on leadership and organizational structures – for they seemed to be refreshing and paradigm breaking enough themselves. A time of compromise started. I worked with a new yet conformational form of leadership; it was exciting because of the platform it created and the response it received, but it still felt somewhat half-baked.

It was time to get real. I could feel it and it was as if I could hear it loud and clear: 'Compliance is false. Settling for the pseudo-comforts of the known just delays what wants to be born anyway. It is time to surrender to the wish of the true and authentic self. Only that can add growth to this planet, its people, organizations... life itself. Only that will be worth following.' The little voice in the back of my mind was blessed with a clear whisper.

And this is what the voice (and pen) started adding to it: 'Nothing out there can change politics, people's way of thinking or behaving. No books, ideologies, leadership seminars, master coaches... The real solutions to radical change are within each and every one of us. They are within you. It's you that you have been waiting for. It always has been you. This is not a concept. It becomes real when you have the courage to pause, look within and find the passionate fire that wants to burn away the shackles from your imprisoned authentic you. Take down your masks of belonging, pleasing, controlling. Address the fears that keep any masks in place, the fears that keep you encaged in your comfort zone. Then inquire what makes your heart tick, what gives you that childlike excitement. That which feels alive is the door to true passion and purpose. Anything less is a compromise, a settling for ways of the known. This is dead. Live and experience the passion, and leadership comes alive. People "have to" follow. Passionate expression of the true authentic self is contagious.'

There was no way around it. I just 'had to' stop, listen, and take action. It was time to explore *leadingship*.

AUTHENTICITY

& PASSION

IN CHARGE

1. 7 Billion leaders, 7 billion followers

7 Billion unique people and you think that only a small percentage has true leadership qualities? Think again!

7 Billion unique people and you think your IQ, EQ, skin color, physical strength, heritage, gender, money, religion or spiritual experience gives you the unique right to a leadership position? Think again!

Science seems to point out how we are all essentially built of the same energy, matter and space. We should therefore all be individuals led and fed by the same universal principles. So how can there only be a select few with the 'right' mix of qualities to lead? And why is it that most of us are looking up to these few people to direct our lives, to shape our destiny?

Interesting questions, aren't they?

This is what seems to take place over and over again. We feel inspired by some people; we start to aspire the qualities and actions that we admire in them. We call it charismatic, inspirational, servant, integrative, authentic, conscious, intuitive or even spiritual leadership. And we conceptualize it as the one true leadership that can be taught and learned.

But this immediately raises another question: If there was such a thing as the one true leadership, don't you think we would have stopped looking for newer and better versions of leadership by now? It should have taken care of all the challenges the world is being faced by on a political, economic, social and environmental level.

We also seem to have decided that the one true version of leadership is only available to a minority of people with the 'right' background, intelligence, skills and experience. And the majority submits to this. Until this moment, leadership known to mankind has been based on a majority looking at a 'higher ranked' minority to lead the way. So even though we all have access to unique and inspiring qualities, we attribute more meaning to a minority who has decided to express them.

We just seem to be staring in the wrong direction!

What makes us decide to follow someone's lead? We feel inspired by that person's action or words. Yet, not just any action or words inspire us. There must be some form of conscious or subconscious recognition of it. We need to have a certain reference to it so that it can resonate within. If there are no seeds in the soil, we can add sunlight, water and fertilizer to it, but nothing will grow.

When someone inspires us by the passionate expression of their authentic genius, it feels like he or she is speaking to some latent part in us, something that we recognize to be true. 'Recognize' comes from the Latin word 'recognare'. 'Re' means 'again', 'cognare' means 'knowing'. You just know it again i.e. you already know it. This true unique genius is part of you, otherwise it couldn't be recognized.

So why would you decide that the expression of your authentic genius is less than anyone else's? Who are you to say no to your innate qualities that want to be used by life? What gives you the right to squander any possible inspiration that can be born through you?

We live in a fantastic world that offers everything for everyone.

Whatever you want to do or create, there are the means to do it. Why wait? Tomorrow might not happen – your heart can stop beating, a tsunami or earthquake might strike... Instead of settling for some compromised version of you, there is a great opportunity to let you, your family, friends, colleagues, organization and even the world benefit from your unique qualities right now.

You are one of 7 billion leaders.

•

You are one of 7 billion followers.

2003, Rotterdam. Musical artist Prince performs in a sold-out Ahoy. After about 45 minutes of stunning entertainment and high quality music, Prince asks the crowd: 'Whom of you is a leader?' Everyone raises their hand screaming 'me!' Prince chuckles, slightly confused. This apparently wasn't the response he anticipated. Tentatively he approaches the microphone again and says: 'So who will follow me?' He touched on the essential element of following.

Some of us might recognize the innate authentic potential within. Some of us might even decide to express it in a passionate way because we experience how it inspires others. And then it begins...

This newly born dynamic of leading and following temporarily maneuvers us in a position of power and admiration often accompanied by a bigger paycheck and a higher status – and we like it. What we like, we want to hold on to. To be more specific: when something makes us feel good, our ego can get attached to it; it wants to maintain the situation that sparked off this good feeling.

Translated to leadership: ego wants to keep the personified leadership alive, by re-establishing the position (with all its material and immaterial benefits) that was spontaneously created in the past. And because it was in the past, it's dead, it's no longer here. The only way to hold on to something from the past is by some version of control – which, as history and the current social-economic climate seem to show us, is a recipe for confusion, friction and misunderstanding.

Unfortunately, more often than not, leadership dynamics seem to get tainted by ego's appetite for personal gain. Before we know it, our ego has told us that who we are and what we do deserves a leadership position. Only ego can take credit for the unique qualities that come with our birth.

Ask yourself this: if these qualities were 'given' to you and their expression make others follow, who or what is really the leader? Only ego can create segmentation and hierarchy between the authentic expressions of individuals. Because: is a German baker's bread less inspiring than Gandhi's prayer for truth and non-violence? Is a tear-jerking blockbuster performance by an Oscar winning actor worth more than your baby's heart-warming smile?

Your unique qualities can only inspire others when these people take time to experience them. This temporary interaction of leading and following is based on the expression AND recognition of unique qualities that are inspiring and appropriate in that moment. No leading without following. As a matter of fact: how can you know leading, if you never follow?

•

Since my first interest in leadership dynamics I have been experiencing how ego has been the ink in clear water. A leadership dynamic that was born out of a pure, passionate expression of authentic qualities, soon got translated to some repeatable version which had a group of people looking at one person for ongoing inspiration.

On a macro-level it has meant that minorities tried to find ways to stay in the saddle – and reap the benefits that come with it. Meanwhile the majority tried to justify why they are turning to those leaders for answers rather than inquiring what innate authentic qualities could be expressed.

It has never felt sustainable and it seems like the world's stage for economy, politics and fashionable spirituality is reflecting that more and more.

It's been the reason for me to stop consuming any version of leadership and let myself jump 'down the rabbit hole' of *leadingship*. So far I have experienced that in *leadingship* the ego has nothing to cling to. Leading and following play an equally important part. That in itself requires trust in ourselves, in others and in the intelligent force that has created all of us and everything.

Leadingship challenges us to let go of control and to let go of the assumed benefits that might come with traditional leadership. It invites us to leave the idealized concept of the established order and structures behind us. *Leadingship* cannot be kept to a few particular forms; it's governed by life itself. Life is change: time moves on, form gets created and dies continuously. So why would leading and following be rigid?

Leadingship knows 7 billion leaders and 7 billion followers who can engage in limitless dynamics of inspiring and being inspired.

Self-inquiry:

If this unique form that is you would like to be expressed, what would it look like? If you no longer compared yourself with others, ranking where you stand in relation to them, but instead made way for what is true and authentic in you – who would you be, what would you do? Who or what would you follow? How would you be used to inspire others?

2. Authenticity versus copy-paste

When we explore what we admire in inspiring leaders, authenticity seems to be one of the highest values. Any other characteristics can only truly be admired if laden in authenticity. I therefore started inquiring what people mean by authenticity – in books, studies and research. In general I have come across lists of qualities: true, pure, spontaneous, reliable, original, open... perhaps a few more like compassion, integrity and transparency.

In my training programs and coaching I have asked professionals if they knew what authenticity meant. They all said they do. Authenticity to them was highly inspiring and an essential element to leadership. So I assumed that authentic leadership was common good. But I was surprised. When asked 'Are you one hundred percent authentic in your action and expression one hundred percent of the time?' no one has ever said 'yes'. How can this be? We seem to know the value of authenticity in leadership. We seem to know what it encompasses. So how come we don't put it into practice?

Let's take a further look at what defines authenticity and how we can recognize it. Instead of going into a technical description of it, I will merely speak from direct experience.

•

Somehow it seems easier to define authenticity by what it's not. I recognize it when someone's actions or words are not authentic. How? I can sense it. It doesn't feel true, spontaneous, original or open. It's as if that specific person is only presenting a certain image of him or herself. I experience it to be somewhat false and my body gives the signals to confirm it.

Therefore when someone does speak or act authentically I can experience it as true. This is why I started relating to authenticity as 'the embodied reflection of truth'. To me truth is the essence of life. It's unlimited, always changing, all-inclusive, inspiring and simple. Authentic behavior reflects that. Especially when spontaneity, originality and simplicity show up, to me it's a good indication for authenticity. It also looks like the behavior and words suit the person very well in that moment - as if they are a pure representation of his or her unique qualities right there right then. And... it just feels good!

I can relate to that feeling when I experience children, especially the younger ones. They can randomly and unexpectedly dance, run, mimic fighting scenes or sing songs to the imagined big crowd. I love it because it feels so unobscured by behavioral rules. Seeing a kid throw a big tantrum is like drinking a very tasty fizzy drink – it makes me giggle with the unbridled energy that's being tossed around. Once, at London Heathrow, queuing up for customs, a kid whom I never met before pulled on my pants. I went down on one knee to check what she wanted. She told me eye to eye that she loved me. What else can you do other than melt?

At a young age we don't know any other way to be than authentic. Most of our (inter)actions are spontaneous, contagious and inspiring. The older we get, the more we learn what is supposedly 'stupid', 'weird' and 'inappropriate'. So our window of authentic expression becomes smaller and smaller. When we are old enough to engage with some leadership position, we already know that we 'need' to lead by example; and that example is defined by a limited set of qualities and behaviors. We hope that by sticking to them we will get the result we aimed for: people following our lead. Especially when we might have picked and tasted the sweet fruits once, we keep repeating it while expecting the same outcome. I call it 'copy-pasting'.

We copy-paste a socially conditioned and accepted version of authentic leadership into the next moment, and the next, and the next...

Copy-pasting is the exact opposite of authenticity. And unfortunately copy-pasting seems to have become the norm. This is the exact reason why people in leadership positions can only admit not to be authentic one hundred percent of the time. As leaders we are trying to re-apply some leadership strategy that proved successful in the past. And deep down we know that we are somehow compensating, compromising, covering up our true authentic self.

In my training programs and coaching sessions, leaders have recognized that kind of compromise, that limitation of true expression. They have named countless forms of conditioned behavior that are in the way of authentic expression and lead to copy-pasted leadership behavior. It's considered 'normal' to have that kind of censorship in place.

Somehow throughout our personal and professional lives we inherit negative belief systems that condemn authentic expression. We learn what is socially and culturally accepted and what might subject us to any form of active or passive repercussion. In due time, being authentic has become something worth aspiring to as long as it fits within our conditioned frame of reference.

And this is what makes it intriguing on a slightly philosophical level. This frame of reference by definition doesn't allow authenticity. It's a frame and therefore limited. If authenticity is an embodied reflection of truth and if truth is unlimited, how can any behavior born from such a frame be authentic?

•

I have heard people in leadership positions say: 'I am authentic most of the time; what you see is what you get.' On the surface it sounds quite real. The question is: is that behavior still regimented by some form of censorship? Or are you totally free in your actions and words no matter what the consequences might be? That question has often been met with a counter question: 'But you can't always be spontaneous, intuitive or transparent because…' Whatever has come after the word 'because', it has always been a great start for exploration! And from my direct experience I can say: everyone has come to a similar conclusion.

Somehow we learn that true authentic behavior is not always understood, liked or condoned. We decide – consciously or subconsciously - to alter our behavior hoping for more listening and understanding. But this compensation of our true authentic self essentially does not feel good, free or open – to us or to others. It therefore defeats the object of leadership: inspiring someone else.

Another comment I have heard in this context is: 'My team knows that I'm simply a dedicated, serious, no-bullshit kind of person.' There's nothing wrong with dedication or seriousness. The question is: is it authentic and inspiring in each and every moment? It can't be! There will be situations requiring some lighter qualities in leadership, but the window of authentic expression has been narrowed down. That what's truly being asked for in the leader is not available, because his or her conditioned programming doesn't allow it.

On the cover of a business magazine, I saw the picture of a highly regarded politician. The quote underneath her unhappy face: 'I'm not in this position to be liked, I'm here to get results.' Ouch! Only copy-pasting some learned or conditioned way of leading can sustain that kind of communication. It definitely cannot be authentic, as in truth we all want to connect and be liked some time, don't we? And how inspiring do such words actually feel?

It does raise another question: How do anger and authenticity relate to each other in the context of leadership? To this day I have never heard any leading professional mention 'anger' as a qualification of authentic leadership. We often judge anger and definitely its expression. So we can try to avoid it, cover it or transmute it into something like disappointment or frustration.

Well, have you ever experienced someone in a leadership position being slightly 'disappointed' with your work? It looked like he or she was trying very hard to be a compassionate, under-standing and communicative leader. And could you actually feel nothing but anger underneath those words and actions? Didn't you just wish that he or she let the authentic anger come up and out? It would have felt much more true and possibly inspiring even, wouldn't it?

What is true for anger is also true for something like 'playfulness'. How many leaders have we heard linking 'playfulness' and 'authenticity'? And yet...

I have experienced a director being very playful during a very important meeting. This specific meeting would determine whether the company would keep a big contract or not. The rest of our team felt embarrassed by his 'immature' behavior, even though his sense of humour was quite contagious. The client's team at the table relaxed, laughed and enjoyed the human inter-action. The contract was renewed without any negotiation.

When I was managing a team in New Zealand I called a meeting wanting to establish team spirit, joint responsibility and focus – and I 'knew' that this needed a serious approach. Looking into the eyes of about ten employees I found nothing but hollow acceptance and compliance. The working days following that meeting were long, the productivity and inspiration low. A week later I spontaneously let myself joke around, having fun. Immediately the whole team joined in. That day we had one of the highest turnovers of the year.

Authenticity cannot be limited to any quality. The needs of each moment are different and therefore the form in which leadership is wanted can be entirely different as well. Anger might be needed to shake up a community that has been asleep to the truth of their situation. Playfulness might cut through the conditioned professional seriousness that is causing stagnation rather than creation.

So are we willing to let go of our rigid idea of who we are – as authentic people and leaders? Are we willing to explore what else is available through us when we consciously allow the window of authentic expression to open up?

•

This is what it all seems to boil down to: any taught and studied version of authentic leadership cannot be authentic. While we copy-paste the studied actions to the situation at hand, we don't leave room for the authentic response that might be needed.

When we look at leadership at a more basic level, we can only come to the same conclusion. The only thing in life that is constant is change. Therefore our professional and personal environments are subject to change all the time. So how can applying a preconceived version of authentic leadership to any situation be effective or sustainable?

For an effective and sustainable dynamic of leading and following it seems to be required that we allow true authenticity to come out and play. True authenticity feels good. It is simple. And it doesn't cost a lot of energy. How can it? It is as close as possible to the truth of who we really are. It has no limitations, it appreciates any other reflection of truth and it knows exactly when to lead and when to follow.

Self-inquiry:
Make a list of the authentic qualities that you recognize in yourself. When you seem to have finished the list, ask yourself: 'Are there any qualities that I might have shied away from that need to be on this list too?'... Then ask someone else (your friend, partner, colleague, parent) what authentic qualities they recognize in you... Is their list longer or shorter than your own? What conclusion can you draw?

3. Passion: the emotional compass

I have come to understand that authenticity doesn't stand alone in the dynamic of leading and following. There is another key-element to inspiration: passion.

The word passion knows many connotations. My relationship with it is quite basic. Whenever I feel truly moved or emotionally touched by something and when it then feels like an uncontrollable fire is ignited within, I start using the word passion. When it feels so good that it almost 'needs' to be shared or put into action, I talk about passion. When I get asked about my secret dreams and wishes and when I imagine them having manifested in my life, I feel extremely warm, excited like a child and as if energy wants to burst out through the skin; this I call passion. When a deep, positive emotional desire to do, have, or be something or someone arises, passion is in play.

Bottom line: passion is often emotionally overwhelming, very compelling and it feels extremely good.

So here we have it: passion is intertwined with two of seemingly the most dreaded words in the context of leadership: 'feeling' and 'emotions'. Whenever I start mentioning these words in leadership clinics or training programs it's seldom received with a lot of enthusiasm or understanding. Why would it? There's no time to check how we might feel; we need to be efficient in meeting the targets. We need to keep a clear mind, make decisions that are not influenced by any emotional state. Even admitting as leaders that we might be troubled by some emotions can be perceived as weak and not having 'it' together. And don't we just leave our personal 'problems' (i.e. emotions) at home anyway?

So I ask them: 'Does it cost energy to keep your emotions out of the way? Or does it give you energy?'

Of course, it's a rhetorical question! This is why. Just look at the word 'emotion'. Put a hyphen between 'e' and 'motion'. What does E stand for in physics? Energy. Emotion is energy in motion. Having explored and taught emotional personal growth work around the world for years, I can honestly not come up with a better description than the one that a dear friend offered to me: energy in motion.

When I look at Wikipedia or any other dictionary, when I open books or websites on molecular biology and read all the technical phrases, my head starts aching. Because so much research has gone into the physiological or psychological side of emotions it seems like we have lost track of the simple non-personal beauty of it.

Emotion: energy in motion. How can we say no to emotions in any context, when it's non-personal energy coming through the body?

In our society we seem to judge which emotions are okay to be expressed and which not, depending on the time and place where they come up. But have you ever experienced how anger and creative power can feel very similar? Did you ever cry with joy? Have you loved someone so much it hurts? How can you truly know which is what? Energy is boundless, in its quantity and form. And we expect our brain to come up with the right labels for what we feel!

It's only logical that trying to separate ourselves from emotions will cost energy. First, we try to determine what emotion we are actually feeling, which costs time and energy. Then, after we have judged and labeled the emotion and have decided that it's not welcome right now, we need to push the emotion away, keep it at bay or make it look and feel like something more presentable. This costs energy.

It's so ironical: no matter how hard we try, this energy comes through the body whether we want it or not. Having worked on 5 continents with people from different countries, cultures, religions, skin colors and professional backgrounds, I have never met anyone who was able to actually control emotions. Sure, we can try to hide or exaggerate them. We can even try to transmute them into a more socially accepted form. However, the energy itself seems to decide whether it wants to be experienced or not.

•

There's another aspect to our emotional field of experience that often seems to remain unaddressed. Throughout human existence our emotional response to situations and interactions has been conditioned. We have learned that feeling and expressing emotions – we call them 'our' emotions' – is often not a good idea. But while we decide against these feelings our whole existence seems to be running on discernment between what feels good or doesn't feel good. In a way it's not very different from how we recognize something or someone to be authentic or not.

Imagine something that is high on your wish list. It can be the next step in your career, a favorite kind of car or house, it can be a new dimension to your relationship or a holiday that you've always wanted. How do you know that that's what you would like to experience? It just feels good, doesn't it? Even if you have plenty of rational reasons to back up your wish, you can only truly relate to it when you imagine having it and then feel the positive energy coming through the body. The opposite is also true. When something isn't right for you the body experiences certain signals. We just labeled these signals as frustration, anger, sadness, fear, panic or just as 'it doesn't feel good'.

No matter how you look at it, feelings i.e. emotions are part of our daily experience of life – be it in our private environment or in our career. They act as some kind of compass, telling you which direction feels good and which one doesn't. So can there be any logical reason to exclude them from your engagements, decisions and interactions?

Because it doesn't seem that natural in our western professional society to listen to our 'gut', I've learned to offer slightly more practical approaches.

I love movies! They create all these immense feelings, even though I fully realize the triggers are on a two-dimensional screen; I'm not in the actual situation of fighting, crying, laughing and running. Still it 'feels' real enough.
And: have you ever thought about something in your life that you are really uncomfortable with? It brings up some form of fear, doesn't it? When that situation actually does happen, similar fear shows up, doesn't it?

In the scientific realms it's been common knowledge that the body reacts to imagined situations pretty much the same way as it does to real time situations. And that is a fantastic given. It means we've got a tool to let ourselves be guided in which step to make now... and now.... and the next moment. I use it in pretty much all my decisions – it determines whether I grab a beer or a glass of water, whether I start writing a new chapter or take the dog out for a walk, whether I engage in a professional relationship with someone or not. Sometimes I forget or decide not to follow this compass and I pay the price for it!

nice
example

I once met a German economic analyst from a multinational company who jumped into total resistance when he heard this. He 'knew' that in order for him to come up with the right calculations to support a decision, he had to shutdown and push away any emotional experience – it could only interfere. I asked him if he had been cracking his brain over a big professional decision recently. He said yes. So I asked if he was willing to explore an alternative. He was. I just asked him to imagine having chosen option A and then to check how the body responded to it – was it a good feeling or did it feel tense, tight? Then I let him imagine having chosen option B. Again I asked him to check his body for any responses. He smiled.

What he understood was how he had learned to keep delving into mind to find the right answers. Calculation after calculation and still he wasn't 100% sure. His body though gave him very clear signals through emotional experience. He then started wondering why he had to use calculations in the first place; he was doubting the raison d'être of mind. This is where I had to draw a certain line.

The point is not to exclude anything. The point is to include everything!

Mind is an amazing tool when used for the appropriate situations. And this is also true for emotions. Instead of pushing away our emotional signals, why not listen to them? Instead of wasting our energy and time on shutting down to this kind of energy, we can be much more efficient and let it 'do some of the work' for us.

And the only thing that is truly needed is your decision to allow emotions into your private and professional life. More energy can be available to you and it can be much easier to experience the inspirational power of authenticity and passion.

•

Back to passion. When I meet someone who is very passionate about life or work, I feel inspired. When I am passionate about something it feels good, I experience life (or work) to be easy and fun and people feel inspired by it. So when passion shows up as a very positive emotional impulse, could there be any reason not to follow it?

My life has been marked by a series of big changes of direction, chosen very spontaneously yet consciously. Friends, family, colleagues and many other people have felt compelled to comment on it. 'Adventurous', 'daring', 'courageous', 'inspiring' and 'you're really doing what you like' is what I've heard. However, it's not been the only feedback. Many times the radical changes have been met with resistance, judgment, not under-standing and even anger. Interesting, isn't it?

Every single big life-change I've made has been fuelled by passionate energy moving through the body. Somehow it felt like this couldn't be ignored, like it was bigger than me, quite overwhelming and uncontrollable. The internal compass was blatantly pointing in a different direction. And who am I to not trust it? Every time I didn't follow that kind of childlike excitement I got very disappointed in life, felt as if life was heavy, pressing down on me. Every time I did listen, I got spoiled with many amazing surprises. It always exceeded any expectations I might have had. It taught me the insignificance of any fears I had of being judged or rejected by my social environment.

Now, whenever something triggers the passion, I stop, assess my personal and professional life and decide to try out this thing that is linked to the passion. Somehow this new path might seem unknown and yet something deep inside of me recognizes it. Walking those first few steps onto the 'Yellow Brick Road' makes me feel like I'm fully in tune with life itself. It fires up many positive emotional responses in the body and I feel like I want to share this with as many people as I can.

People recognize the expression of this passion; it inspires them, at least for a while. I often hear what a lucky man I am, how exciting it is that I just keep living life in such an adventurous way and how amazing it is that I get successful every time. And then something else kicks in and people tell me how they would like to live life in the same way but how they can't because of… All the reasons I have heard have felt serious, heavy, constraining, negative. And right there right then I see people choose status quo, compromise, the seemingly 'safe' environment of the known – all great seedbeds for stress, burnout, depression, definitely not for inspiration, creation, efficiency, productivity.

And here is the key question. Something in life is triggering passion, and you can feel it. It somehow wakes up the recognition of new opportunities even if you can't see the actual form yet. You know how you've been inspired by leaders who are authentic and passionate about what they do. You've experienced how giving expression to the passion inside of you has inspired you and others. Whenever passion comes through the body it seems to be bigger than you, uncontrollable and it just feels good. So why would there, privately or professionally, be any reason to not follow this passion? Why would you deny this opportunity to be led to new horizons and inspire others by it?

Welcoming emotions into the dynamics of leading and following means that we allow energy to come through the body, from which we can only benefit. By doing so we get a clearer sense of what feels good and what doesn't. Our internal compass leads the way, it tells us each moment whether to sit tight and let others take charge or to step up to the plate and let the authentic qualities that are available in us to be shared.

By saying 'yes' to the emotional aspect of our interactions the body will be more prone to passion coming through. This is the uncontrollable, positively overwhelming energy in motion that wants to be reckoned with – it asks us to stop, listen, take action and enjoy. It will feel inspiring to us and will therefore be inspiring to others, pretty much without us having to do anything. Passion is a real head turner, it's a luring beauty that cannot be overlooked or denied.

Responding to passion can create the most inspiring professional and personal steps in life. It actually makes life very exciting, surprising, effortless, energetic and fun. So why would you not follow it and lead the way?

Self-inquiry:
What things in life have you ever felt passionate about? Name even those things that you have been hiding from others and yourself... If life could highlight one or two things that are still worth pursuing, which ones would that be?... Now imagine having followed that passion and having put these things into action, how does it feel?... Imagine being surrounded by your partner, friends, family and colleagues. They are witness to you having followed this passion; how do they react?... Now that you've taken these new steps in your life, what other doors are opening, what else is possible?...

THE ILLUSION
OF CONTROL

4. The feared unknown

Authenticity is inspiring. As an embodied reflection of truth it's limitless and ever changing. It wants expression so that the unique qualities can be used in the grant dynamic of non-personal leading and following. And above all: it feels good.

Why on earth would we still put a bridle on it? What makes us decide to cover up, hide, overcompensate or deny the authentic qualities that are available in each and every individual? Can there be any valid reason to believe and decide that someone's unique set of qualities is better or worse than someone else's?

Following the call of passion is inspiring, exciting, energetic and fun. It allows us to engage with a new experience. And above all: it feels good.

Still, when this passion arises in our field of experience and tries to guide us to something new, we decide to stay put. We come up with all the 'logical' reasons why not to follow this pull right now. Meanwhile this unique chance for change, growth, inspiration and leadership is passing us by. Later on in our career or life we regret not having taken the leap. So what happened?

•

The only reason not to follow the passion and to keep an expression of our authentic qualities limited to the socially accepted norms, seems to be control – to be more specific: the control of our comfort zones.

Control is a funny thing. The word and the energy that comes with it immediately evokes resistance, in me as well. I've tried to start writing this part of the book many times. Somehow I got stopped in my tracks straight away. Every sentence got checked with an immediate and very serious editing.

Whenever I have addressed control in a leadership training or coaching session, people have tried to convince me that there is nothing wrong with control – especially when they were in an established leadership position! I've even heard highly regarded spiritual and political leaders state that some form of control is justifiable in certain situations. The exploration of control has resulted more than once in serious discussions that don't seem to end.

As far as I can tell, there is a clear reason why there seems to be hesitance and resistance when exploring the truth of control: control knows so many faces and is so pervasive that we can't see the forest for the trees. We all use control in so many different forms. We seem to do so to keep ourselves smaller or bigger than who we really are in order to avoid rejection, humiliation, heart-break, deep disappointment, loneliness, hurt, insanity, weakness and many other forms of energy in motion.

Because of our 7 billion lives with 7 billion unique sets of qualities we use many billions of control strategies. And because it's so common, we accept that it's part of our personal and professional lives. We justify the need for control – especially in terms of leadership – because of the (false) sense of security, order and structure it provides and because 'someone needs to be in charge'.

•

When I opened this can of worms for this book, I was walking our dog. The minute I asked myself 'What is the true nature of control?' my dog ran away from me. He is very well trained and behaved, always responds to my whistle. However, not this time. His hunting instinct and superb smell lead him to a dead rabbit. He tore off one leg, looked at me to check what I – the alpha male – would do and decided to start chewing on it.

I called him several times and felt this urgency inside to get him to listen and come back to me. I did not want him to finish off this leg that had been lying there for I don't know how many days. I could already imagine him being sick in our house, us having to go to the vet and even worse. I was genuinely concerned about many things – especially because I didn't know how eating this rabbit's foot would impact him. I was afraid of the consequences I couldn't oversee yet, I was afraid of the unknown.

I started calling him louder and louder, tried to approach him, which he countered with running away from me. I tried becoming very angry in my voice and energy alternated by a sweet voice trying to lure him back to me. Nothing worked. I saw the last bit of leg disappear into this mouth, a few crackling sounds and it was gone. I called him again with a big energy and some anger in my voice. 'He just hadn't listened, and he should.'

He finally came over to me, I put him on the lead and wanted to start walking. For the first time ever, like an alligator, he totally resisted the pull, rolled over a few times and freed himself from the lead. I called him back again, put the collar around his neck and walked away. This time he came along, only instead of being by my side he kept wanting to walk away from me.

I stopped and suddenly realized the synchronicity in it all. I had allowed the thoughts and energy of control into my field of experience: it sparked off all the events. I checked my body and felt how it was contracted with a mix of fear and anger. I checked where my energy was: it was large and forceful, and my dog was still trying to move away from me. I chose to welcome everything without holding onto it; the contraction came and went, the energy diluted and became soft and neutral. And I couldn't believe my eyes: straight away my dog stopped pulling the lead and walked side by side with me, his tail wagging high up in the air. I stopped, took the lead off, asked him to come over, treated him to a big cuddle and gave him permission to run off again, which he gratefully accepted by staying by my side the rest of the walk.

I was willing to acknowledge that my control over him was illusionary. My efforts to make him do what I want in order to feel more secure were in vain. That in itself restored the natural dynamics between him and me. In only a few minutes he inspired me to uncover the true nature of control. His perfect uncontrolled and uncontrollable leadership ignited the inspiration to start this chapter from a whole different angle. Before this event the words that I used in this realm of control were serious and intellectual. That was the illusion of control speaking. Now there is a light approach, it feels simple. It allows control to be explored through the authentic qualities within me and straight away the body experiences an exciting energy, a certain passion that keeps on navigating the fingers on this keyboard.

Self-inquiry:
While walking, sitting or lying down give your body and mind the permission to relax, to give up any control. Feel how the muscles unwind in your forehead, face, neck, shoulders, arms, chest, belly, back, lower back, groin, legs, ankles and feet. Take a deep breath in and exhale fully. Truly imagine how you let go. When vulnerability or any form of fear shows up, just acknowledge it and give it space to be experienced without doing anything to it. There's no right or wrong, there's only

your experience in this moment. Be willing to experience what happens when you let go of the illusionary control that you might be so used to...

•

After nearly a decade of personal growth and emotional work I uncovered one of the main reasons for control. We all seem to have one big underlying fear: the fear of death i.e. non-existence of our physical form, our mind and our emotional connection. We can't know death until we have experienced it; it's unknown to us, which brings up fear. We all seem to be subject to fear of the unknown. And we seem to have agreed that control might be the only way to deal with it. And this also seems to be the case when it comes to authenticity and passion.

Our social environment is suffused with control. In every environment there is a definite copy-paste version of how we should or shouldn't be. Jumping outside that culturally and socially conditioned bandwidth puts us at risk – we might get judged, rejected, punished, ridiculed, dumped or fired. Because we can't actually know what the response will be, we decide to move away from the fear (of the unknown) that comes with it. We settle for some pseudo comfort, something that makes us feel 'safe'.

Instead of allowing the true authenticity to come out and play, instead of letting ourselves be spontaneously led by passion, instead of becoming an inspiration to ourselves or others, we control our actions, words and even thoughts. We create a bubble of comfort in which we allow a limited expression of who we really are. It's called a comfort zone. Needless to say that this comfort zone, and the control that comes with it, is counter productive to any expression of the authentic leadership that *leadingship* demands.

We all seem to recognize this. When people are asked what qualities they truly admire in their favorite leaders, breaking the mould gets named, as well as standing for what they believe in, being non-conformational. We feel inspired by human beings who courageously burst out of their comfort zones. But do we follow that lead and let ourselves be inspired to burst out of our own comfort zones?

Have you ever experienced not being happy in your job? All emotional signals pointed out that it was time to quit, but because of your mortgage, family situation, relationship and many other reasons you decided to hang in there. How did it feel? Did it inspire you? Were your interactions at work filled with fun, laughter, inspiration and creation? Did you feel productive and energetic? Or was the experience quite the opposite?

On the other hand, have you ever experienced a time when passion was ignited by the possibility of a new career move? Even though you might not have seen or experienced the actual job, something inside of you responded very clearly to this new opportunity. And you chose to follow it. How did that feel? Exciting, somewhat scary? Was there even a clear distinction between the excitement and fear? Could you feel the adrenalin rush? Did it feel a bit like jumping off the cliffs into the white-capped waves of the ocean below? And once you actually made that leap, what were the consequences of that choice? Did you experience confirmations of this being the right choice, even though your mind tried to doubt it or tried to analyze why you should or shouldn't have jumped?

•

For nearly 7 years I had been representing a company that facilitates personal growth and leadership seminars around the world. About 6 months before this book started to get written, I noticed the negative signals coming through the body whenever I had to focus on my work for this company. However, the promise of a rewarding partnership and an established platform for group work made me choose to stay in my comfort zone. Next to that my personal life seemed to justify this choice for the known: my wife was pregnant, we were converting our loft and we had taken a puppy into our house.

My mind kept telling me that choosing this kind of safety was okay for now. My body kept getting very different signals. Every now and then I decided to entertain the thought of stepping away from this company and launch a company of my own. There was no denial possible: the energy that came through was bubbly, vast, light, focused and solid. Once I had experienced this passionate reaction a few times, I promised myself to at least follow it in my spare time. Outside my working hours for the company I would invest energy in developing my new company, product and of course website. And I felt trapped. After working hours and after not having felt one hundred percent inspired or creative during the day, there was tiredness in the body. I allowed myself to give in to the tiredness and spent relaxation time with my wife or myself. But the passion kept knocking on my door.

In the meantime my work for the company seemed to be accompanied by more and more resistance within me. The building frustration, due to the company not wanting to grow into the direction that I intended, got projected onto the company: I blamed them for not complying with my expectations. The truth of it all was that it was easier to believe the story of frustration than to surrender to the fear of the unknown field of experiences, which the passion wanted to guide me towards. My friends, relatives and even new acquaintances seemed to ask me the same thing: 'Do you really want to keep working for this company? It looks like it's time for you, for something that will allow the true you to work with people and organizations in a different way.'

Controlling myself inside my comfort zone became quite unbearable. It was costing so much energy. But I kept going in the same direction. It wasn't until my back collapsed and I had to stay still when all the built up frustration, anger, disappointment and many other forms of energy were allowed to come through the body in their full dimensions. A day later there was so much clarity and strength showing up in me that the decision to step away from the company was easily made - even though it brought up fear because of saying goodbye to a 'guaranteed' basic income in a time of uncertain economics and new family circumstances. From that moment on I promised myself to always follow the call of passion, to listen to the reflection that life is presenting through people and circumstances – even if I can't see or know what it might bring.

A day after the decision was made, an email found its way into my inbox. An HR director in a Dutch organization knew about my intended launch of *leadingship* training & coaching. She noticed that her department was ready for a shift of paradigm, a new approach to leadership. She filled an A-4 with the intentions and wishes of her department and was wondering if this could be matched with the *leadingship* work. It was the perfect fit.

That same day (and night) I wrote and designed my whole website. There was an understanding that the Dutch organization needed some background information to get the intentions behind *leadingship* training and coaching. The excitement and clarity kept me up all night creating a website that was a unique reflection of the authentic me. The day after, I wrote a proposal for a training and coaching program. Three days later I got a phone call with the whole HR department on speaker. The team was extremely excited to be the first professional guinea pigs of this new *leadingship* work.

Following the passion without any guarantee of income paid off immediately. Once again my trust in the unknown was rewarded. The conscious decision to step outside the old comfort zone opened the doors for new opportunities.

•

Because we fear the unknown social response, we shy away from the authentic expression of ourselves. Because we fear the unknown situational consequences, we often choose not to trust the passionate intelligent force that creates everything. We don't allow ourselves to swim downstream and because of that we experience our private and professional life as challenging.

Do you recognize having gone against the grain of authentic action or passion? Did it feel light or did you experience a certain kind of heaviness? Have you also looked for people, organizations and situations that can be blamed for that heaviness? What were the control-driven beliefs and excuses that made you stick with this heaviness rather than moving along with what makes you feel good? 'The new opportunity might not be for me right now'? 'I can't risk losing my income'? 'Other people have got better qualifications to take up the new challenge'? 'Someone needs to take responsibility'?...

After a while we have invested so much energy in our current comfort zone that letting go of the reins doesn't appear to be an option.

But...

Control is never real. How can it be? Control tries to maintain a status quo in life, while life itself is ever changing.

Letting go of the illusion called control means letting in the unknown. Exploring the unknown asks for humility and innocence. It means allowing some playfulness into your interactions. It means that you don't know whether you will be in the leading or following position the next moment, and the next, and the next... All of a sudden the heavy weight of responsibility fades away and gets replaced by the joy of inspiration, authentic expression and warm passion. It feels good, so it must be worth following. Don't you think?

Self-inquiry:
What comfort zones do you recognize in your personal or professional life? How specifically have you kept yourself locked in out of fear of certain social responses or situational consequences? Pick one that you feel the strongest emotional reaction to... Now ask yourself: what do I perceive to be the highest risks of stepping outside that comfort zone?... Then ask yourself: 'Can I be absolutely certain that this will happen?'

5. Being in charge

Some of us might understand the illusion of control. However, when alternative words for control come into play, words that are very common in leadership dynamics, our judgment might get clouded. Just think of 'being in charge' and 'responsibility'. Aren't they considered perfectly acceptable in terms of leadership?

Time to take a closer look, starting with 'being in charge'.

First of all, we like to believe that we are in charge of our own lives. Whenever I hear this confirmed, my question is: 'Oh really? So birth happens without you influencing it… but you are in charge? Your body might decide to stop breathing right now or you might get killed in a car accident today… but you are in charge? This year the world might be shaken up by the biggest earthquake ever and millions of lives might be taken… but you are in charge?'

Sure, you might have made a choice and as a consequence something might have occurred. This causality might have been expected based on your previous experience. But can you know it to be true that you had full control over what happened; were you really in charge?

•

When it comes to social structures we definitely seem to have a belief system in place that supports the idea of being in charge. Take families for instance. We learn that in family situations parents are in charge. And no one seems to question it. It's just the way things are. You do what your parents tell you to do, because they are 'in control'.

There's no control without the means to control. Unfortunately many parents seem to use forceful language and energy to assert their control over their children. Other parents apply manipulation for the same purpose. My stomach turns every time I experience a child being punished or manipulated verbally, physically, emotionally or mentally because of mummy's of daddy's fear of losing control over their children's actions.

I have experienced both punishment and manipulation to be equally controlling. They both embody a man-made causality: if you do A, I will respond by doing B. And with it comes an energy of threat, no matter how forceful or seemingly sweet. To cover both versions of control I will use the word 'repercussion'.

Time after time I experience how repercussion stands in the way of true inspiration. The people I meet in my *leadingship* training and coaching state the intention to unleash more of their true potential. They generally receive a three-way support: the recognition of their authentic qualities, recognition of the true call of passion and uncovering what might be blocking the passionate expression of those authentic qualities. In the exploration of those blocks they often come across memories of their parents' repercussion to some unwanted behavior. They experience it as one of the main reasons to keep the true expression of who they want to be at bay.

As parents we justify any form of repercussion because children should just do as they're told. We think that this is the way to keep our children safe and secure, because we 'know what's best for them and because we are in charge of their lives until they reach adulthood'. And before we know it we have created a rigid leadership system in which our focus is on the things that aren't going 'right'. We turn to repercussion and highly controlled prevention rather than celebrating and enjoying all the things that are good and beautiful.

'My father never told me he loved me, I never knew if he was proud of me.' I have heard this spoken so many times – not even in a dramatic way, but with a tone of voice that expressed acceptance and resignation. Yet, isn't our father one of the first people we turn to for inspiration and leadership?

Self-inquiry:
Ask yourself how many times you expressed disapproval towards your child or partner simply because he or she did something that scared you. When you imagine yourself being back in those situations, how does it feel to you? And what was the unspoken reaction you could sense?...
Now ask yourself how many times you faced your kid or partner eye to eye and told him or her what you truly love and appreciate, what makes you really proud. How did it feel to do that and what was the response like?...

•

Our society seems to be dominated by a copy-paste version of parenthood that assumes parents being in charge of their kids' lives. And yet, children break away continuously. No matter what age, they make decisions of their own that might shatter the borders of our family comfort zone. At a young age they tend to be explorers in a boundless world of exciting new experiences. It might mean suddenly running across a street, getting stung by this intriguing buzzing thing called 'bee' or burning their hand on the interesting woodstove. As parents we get confronted with the fact that we can't control life and our child's experience of it, no matter how much we think we are in charge.

Sometimes our kids' authentic qualities keep coming out very passionately in a way that is unfamiliar to us. This behavior doesn't always fit in our family comfort zone. We start labeling it as deviant and look at doctors to diagnose them with some behavioral disorder. Such a diagnosis puts our parental mind at ease; it creates this sense of having been 'right' all along about our child being different. But… could it be that we were actually proven wrong? Could it be possible that our illusion of being in charge was shattered by the reality of our kid's true authentic expression?

Because of our vast exploration of this kind of human control and conditioning, my wife and I consciously chose not to be in charge of our daughter's life: we decided to take care of her. We are fully aware how the intelligent life force created such a perfect little human being from only one egg and a sperm cell. We weren't in charge of her development then and we still aren't now. We can give input, breastfeed her and tickle her senses, and yet we can't make her body respond to it. Just like we can't make her stop crying or start laughing.

At times, our daughter's crying seems endless and we know that she has been fed and her nappy has been changed. It can cause this sense of not knowing 'what's wrong' and it can stir up a feeling of inadequacy or fear. It doesn't feel comfortable. That's when we truly understand that we are not in charge; we are mere custodians trying to accommodate her needs as best as we can. And sometimes we fail. This realization puts a smile on our faces; only our arrogant ego-driven minds can create an artificial pressure of being in charge of something that is simply too intelligent for any control.

Self-inquiry:
Ask yourself very honestly: How much have I really been in charge of my own or anyone else's life? See what happens when you become very discerning…

•

So how does this translate to the professional arena? Well, my experience is that it's not that different. After all, our social systems get translated from our private lives to our professional lives and vice versa. The common factor is human being, so it's only natural to assume similarities. And of course it might look a bit different from the outside, simply because we tend to adapt our behavior to the circumstances of the system.

Today's general assumption seems to be that within any kind of organization some defined individual should be in charge. 'You can't have too many captains on a ship' is a favorite expression of many. Of course this kind of reasoning is based purely on the principles of a rigid hierarchical leadership structure. To justify this concept you need the establishment of a majority waiting for a minority to take decisions. You need a minority asserting control to 'make' the majority follow their lead.

When tyranny is displayed on a macro-level we are very quick to judge it. We love demanding justice when some politician has transformed from a promising democrat to a murdering dictator. The question is though: how did it get that far? It's only when the 'person in charge' turns to means of control that he or she can keep re-establishing a leadership position. When the majority keeps agreeing to that kind of punishment and manipulation, believing in the system of one man or woman being in charge, the perfect climate is born to feed such dictatorship.

Take a look at dynamics on a micro-level and we will find the exact same assumptions on who is in charge and what that means. We put someone in charge of a team and attach a job description and therefore expectations to it. It already demands a fixed leadership position and will therefore by-pass any *leadingship* dynamic. By continuously turning to this one person for inspiration and answers, some of the human resources in that group of people will be left unused.

And of course the person in charge needs the team to do what he or she requires to fulfill the job description. In working environments we might recognize that overt controlling leadership doesn't necessarily work. It might even be considered unprofessional. But being in charge means we still want to find a way to influence the group in such a way that they do what we expect. This seems to create a demand for training programs that will teach communication, management or leadership skills. We call it different, it might even look slightly different, but as long as the intention is getting the group to do what we want, it still is control.

•

There's another aspect to putting someone in charge that wants exploring. In our society we are encouraged to follow someone when we can understand his or her action or words. Our cognitive mind tells us whether logically speaking we should accept this kind of leadership or not. At the opposite end of this dynamic we assume that we need knowledge and know-how to be worthy of leading. Until this moment most of our professional structures seem to be built on layers and layers of agreed intellectualized and rationalized concepts and ideas. Our brain i.e. our mind has played a hugely leading part in choosing whom we put in charge or how to stay in charge. But... is mind always worth being in charge?

Ironically I'm referring to a scientific (i.e. mind-fed) approach of this matter. Of course any scientific research can be put to the test; research is simply a recording of that moment and therefore actually out of date the minute it gets published. Research is also based on a hypothesis and therefore subject to the researcher's starting point. Having said that, I have come across particular scientific research that is quite useful in the exploration of how much we trust in the leadership qualities of the cognitive mind.

This particular research has defined a distinction between the conscious mind and the subconscious mind. The conscious mind is considered to be our analytical brain that can make calculations, judgments and discernments. The subconscious mind is considered to make our heart beat, makes us inhale and exhale; it's the intelligent stream of energy that (without us thinking about it) determines how our life takes shape and gets experienced.

Supposedly both minds process information like a computer. This research shows how the conscious mind processes somewhere between 40 and 2000 bits data per second (scientific publications differ a bit, but it doesn't matter for the point that wants to be proven). The subconscious mind apparently processes between 20 billion and 200 billion bits data per second.

In our society - especially in professional environments - intellectual or empirical knowledge are considered gold. We seem to attach a lot of meaning to the conscious mind, so much so that information of the subconscious mind gets overlooked. The conscious mind by nature is highly discerning and thus polarizing – it will doubt anything. Because we put our trust in conscious mind we are naturally inclined to doubt anything that gets communicated by our subconscious mind. That's why the introduction of 'intuition' onto the work floor often gets met with suspicion. Instead we seem to follow any action born from a logical rationalization and understanding.

It means that we keep re-establishing people in leadership positions who have got the IQ, the proven experience and knowledge. We expect them to come up with the right decisions, while this whole system is based on an information stream of only 40 to 2000 bits data per second. Freshly inspiring and intuitive input born from an information stream of 20 to 200 billion bits data per second is by-passed.

This highly intelligent life stream could be in charge – effortlessly, simply and very inspiringly. Its non-personal energy could feed passion to someone's internal compass, which then guides this person to the appropriate use of available authentic qualities, inspiring a new *leadingship* dynamic.

•

Unfortunately we tend to personify the dynamics of leading and following. We expect someone to be in charge. Being in charge is something that is derived from a mutually agreed hierarchy that holds its premise in ratio, intellect and logic.

If our analytical mind tells us that we don't have what it takes to be in charge, we take up the role of follower. Stepping outside our comfort zone carries a risk that we find not worth taking. And we settle for the status quo.

If we find ourselves intellectually and empirically capable enough to lead, we might decide to break through the barrier of the old comfort zone. We enjoy the benefits that come with the spontaneously arisen leadership position. And then the ego-driven need to hold onto it shows up. We become very creative in keeping our emotional and material benefits alive. And to justify it we use the recognized qualities of our conscious mind.

It feels heavy just to read this, doesn't it? It definitely loses the sense of flow and inspiration, so it can't be any indication of *leadingship* in action.

Have you ever experienced the irrational wisdom of a child catching you by surprise? You never looked at it that way, but it actually makes perfect sense. You realize that all these years you have taken something for granted because that's what you learned at school, university or work. This kid's inexperienced and 'naïve' look at it is way more inspiring and feels much more true...

Were the most inspirational people in our history only thinking within the realms of the known and learned? Or is it possible that they innocently surrendered to what the intelligent life force wanted to create or inspire to?

One of the greatest minds – Albert Einstein – is said to have stated:

> 'The only real valuable thing is intuition.
> 'All these primary impulses, not easily described in words, are the springs of man's actions.
> 'Logic will get you from A to B, imagination will take you everywhere.
> 'The most beautiful thing we can experience is the mysterious. It is the source of all true art and science.
> 'There is no logical way to the discovery of elemental laws. There is only the way of intuition, which is helped by a feeling for the order lying behind the appearance.
> 'We should take care not to make the intellect our god. It has, of course, powerful muscles, but no personality.'

I rest my case.

•

As long as we attach any serious meaning to being in charge we lose touch with the effortless, sustainable dynamics of *leadingship*. We have to turn to control to keep the structure of vertical leadership alive. By doing so we choose conditioning over inspiration, repercussion over appreciation, personal intellect over life's boundless intelligence. And: it still doesn't last.

So, why not try something new? Inquire what happens when you bin the illusion of being in charge. How does it affect your private and professional experiences, how do others respond to it? Where does the inspiration come from? Who or what is 'in charge' in any given moment?

6. Responsibility

Being in charge comes with responsibilities, at least that seems to be the assumption in our society. And looking at our verbal language patterns we appear to love responsibility, both privately and professionally – especially in any kind of leadership dynamic. In fact, we are so used to assuming and taking responsibilities that we overlook the negative connotation that is attached to it. The deeper we dive into the realm of responsibility, the more we uncover how this very 'normal', professionally and socially accepted word is defined by contrast, duality and polarization.

It starts when we consult our dictionaries. Words to define and describe responsibility are: answerability, accountability, duty, risk. How can we love or consciously choose that kind of weight on our shoulders? Well, I have come across professionals whose take on it is not that somber. They said that they can even aspire to more responsibility. It puzzled me until I explored this further with them. It was just a matter of semantics. These people didn't necessarily look forward to being held accountable or being at risk. They just aimed for new and perhaps even more interesting challenges. Their intention was to step outside their comfort zone for the purpose of personal growth. And because they were so used to the word 'responsibility' in relation to stepping up the career ladder, they used it to describe their hunger for a new horizon.

Over the last years, more so than not, I have experienced people's allergic reaction to what they see as a professional burden. They might have tasted the sour fruits of increased responsibility, having dealt with the added pressure and stress. Or they might have witnessed family or friends succumb under the heavy weight of it. They have come to understand the threat of being held accountable for other people's actions and non-actions.

When the team we lead doesn't perform as expected, when the results we promised to our superior or shareholder are not met, the pressure is on. We might find ourselves stuck between a rock and a hard place. Not delivering means that our job or company is on the line. But trying to steer the ship onto a better course might mean making decisions that make us less popular with the team we lead. And we need the team to keep the ship afloat.

In the past, we might have felt compensated for this pressure by a bigger paycheck. Extra income was supposed to give us a thicker skin. It would sooth the pain that comes with a blow to the chin. Recently it seems that the phrase 'money doesn't buy you happiness' is winning terrain around the world. I have even heard 'More money, more problems'.

People have described to me the heavy burden of private responsibilities as well. A house, mortgage and family come with responsibilities. They are the main reasons to not follow the passion that is ignited. The true authentic self doesn't get a chance to be expressed; the risk of being rejected, judged or even let go of is just too great. In all truth and honesty we might not want the responsibilities in our private life, because it feels like living a lie and being constrained. But stepping away from them might mean giving up the status, comfort, security and connection that we have grown attached to. Deadlock!

And so it happens. Both privately and professionally the doors can be kept closed because of our negative references to assumed leadership responsibilities. We shut out any new and exciting opportunity for professional growth thinking that this is the only way to maintain a balanced and fulfilling career devoid of any stress. In trying to control our status quo we block the life stream that wants to break through the boundaries of our comfort zone.

And guess what? We justify this control by regurgitating one of society's favorite one-liners: 'You can't just do what you want all the time. Life comes with responsibilities.' Isn't that a fascinating resignation? It would suggest that life without responsibilities is not an option: only death has that privilege. Perhaps this is the reason why the younger generation of professionals gets judged so often. 'They don't seem committed enough, surrendered enough, serious enough. All they want to do is have fun, without having any responsibilities.' We judge what we desire. And we do so by using the r-word.

•

Being held accountable for your team's average performance, having to answer for your own actions despite any possible 'force majeure', feeling the duty that rests on your shoulders or carrying the risk simply because you said yes to something. Because there is this risk attached to being responsible, it seems only logical to take out some metaphorical insurance. So how do we cover ourselves? Blame shifting.

Blame shifting, we do it well; it's become an integral element to our interactions.

When things don't go the way we want, our first inclination is to find someone else to blame: 'Who is responsible for this?' It diverts the attention away from us. When we find that someone, we might say: 'You should take responsibility for your actions' or 'this was your choice so it's your responsibility'.

We know it in our private lives – especially within relationships.

And it's most certainly true for our professional lives. The employer tries to make the employees take their own responsibilities. The employees expect the buck to stop with the employer: he or she is in charge and responsible.

'Responsibility' is the perfect weapon to lash out with or hide behind.

We have been aware of this for quite some time. And because we'd like to avoid the potential power struggle, we have invented rigid job descriptions and contracts. The idea behind it: as long as all the responsibilities are laid out clearly, the system works. In certain professional environments it means that we follow any top down command, no matter what the consequences. 'It wasn't my decision, I'm only following orders…'

Needless to say that there's not a lot of room left for inspiration, authenticity and passion, let alone questioning the integrity of the given order. Vertically controlled leadership thrives by this kind of ranking.

Ranking and responsibility are natural allies against *leadingship*.

•

So it seems that our society values and expects responsibility; its whole structure is based on it. However, that structure is being undermined by our attempt to dodge that same responsibility. We therefore keep erecting a scaffolding of rules, agreed expectations and regulated environments.

In other words, responsibility infuses control.

As long as we can control everyone and everything the risk of being held responsible for any underachievement will be minimal. Our mind therefore creates expectations of how things should be. They are fear-driven projections into the future that give birth to a controlled environment.

So what happens when something doesn't meet the expectation, someone doesn't follow the rules or orders, or a situation bursts through the seams of an established structure...? Here's a telling anecdote that was the actual inspiration for this chapter.

I was asked to give a four-day personal growth seminar to the orthodox Jewish community in Israel. Even though I could rely on a wealth of experience in working with people from all kinds of religious, cultural, ethnic and professional backgrounds, I sensed that it was going to be a very different seminar than I'd given many times before.

For some delegates their version of the religion didn't allow any eye contact or physical contact between men and women. It was decided to have a dividing wall between the male and female delegates. There would be separate entrances. The men's entrance was leading straight onto a busy road. Any male delegate who needed the toilet would therefore automatically cause some kind of disturbance within the seminar room.

The night before the start of the seminar I was briefed about the do's and don'ts in front of this audience. It meant immediately letting go of certain aspects of the intended syntax, which the seminar company that hired me wanted me to follow.

Fifteen minutes before the doors opened I was asked to browse through CD's of religious music that could be used during breaks instead of the English music I would normally pick.

And whatever my personal beliefs, I needed to take a quite neutral stance in my communication, because of the risk of unintentionally offending certain delegates.

I had to let go of (the illusionary idea of) any control. Even though the seminar company expected me to be responsible for the outcome and results, I soon realized that all I could do was react to the requirements of the moment.

The first two days went surprisingly well. But then... Once the paired up delegates had exchanged some deeply personal exercises they were to gather with me for a brief integration. I normally take some time to prepare the room and myself before the session starts. This time the room was already filled with about thirty delegates waiting.

I knew that some men were not allowed to interact with women in the same room, but the group was already mixed. Only two people spoke English, the rest Hebrew. Because the delegates needed a lot of support in their exercises, my translators had been pulled in. It meant that no one was available for translation in the integration room.

I had asked my core support team to arrange consecutive rounds of integration. This would mean no people coming into the room until I was finished with one group. However, the door kept opening continuously and delegates walked in and out as they pleased. The delegates in the room tried to share their experiences and questions with me in their own language, and meanwhile I was hearing from delegates and trainers alike that I needed to speed it all up: a substantial group of people needed to leave very shortly or they would run the risk of not making it back home on time in the occupied territories.

So here I was: trying to get the logistics sorted, to be available for questions that I couldn't understand and to somehow provide the delegates with information that could support the integration of the rather intense seminar day. Needless to say that it got more chaotic by the minute.

All of a sudden I could feel the responsibility grab me by the throat. I feared that the chaos was reflecting on me as the seminar 'leader' and that I had to answer for it. And I felt inadequate in meeting my own and the company's expectations of how this integration should be done. I was totally out of control. And the fuses blew! Anger came up through the body and I was looking for someone to blame and for someone who could restore the order so that I could finally do 'my job' and 'resume the responsibility again'. I walked out of the room and when I finally found one of my core team members I expressed it all. An immediate breach of our very warm and trusting professional relationship was the result. It took at least two full seminar days for this 'fracture' to heal.

When I shared this story afterwards with colleagues and friends, it got met with understanding and even sympathy of my anger. Of course I must have felt angry. The core team, who had supported these seminars before and had been instructed what to do, should have known and done better. Of course I must have felt out of control, but it was not my fault; anyone's fuses would have blown given the circumstances.

There was a belief in the justification for control. With that came the demand that people and situations should live up to certain expectations. Based on my previous experience, the syntax and instructions from the seminar company I had tried to create a controlled environment – even though I was aware from the start that this particular audience was asking for a unique approach. I had stepped away from what wanted to take place authentically. And I had justified it by a credo often expressed by the seminar company: 'creating the highest and best care for the delegates'.

Ego threw a spanner in the *leadingship* wheel. I could have been inspired to new, paradigm breaking action, which would suit the environment and our delegates much better. Instead, I chose status quo and tried to copy-paste previous experience into the present, because 'this is how we do things'.

That night before falling asleep I laughed with the recognition of my ego's need for control. The laughter cracked through the illusion of responsibility. It was a very restful night.

The next morning I was tested straight away. One delegate raised his arm. He was clearly upset and shared why. He had come home later than he anticipated, which had stirred up some unease between him and his partner. Apparently the confirmation of his seminar booking said that the seminar would be finished by 6pm, but he hadn't left the venue before 7. I told him that the time in the confirmation was a genuine mistake and that in other countries we put 8pm in the confirmation. He demanded that I should take responsibility. I paused. I asked him if he could understand that this was totally out of my control: I hadn't been in the loop of any communication that goes on in Israel and I didn't speak or read Hebrew. I asked him if he would be willing to accept my apology for not meeting his expectations. He wasn't. He got even angrier and kept saying how I should take responsibility regardless. I could feel my ego wanting to control the situation as the room of 119 delegates started to become emotionally involved. I, as the seminar leader, was responsible; I needed to re-establish rapport between me, him and all the other delegates…

And I stopped the ego express train that wanted to leave the station. Suddenly I recognized the new test at hand. I chose to pause once more, looked at him and found myself asking very simply: 'Does holding me responsible make you feel good or not?' To express my authentic experience I added that the projection of his anger made me feel physically shaky and I asked him if that was his intention. He was honest enough to say that it didn't feel good to him either. He let his attention go to his body and said that he experienced how his body was burning with anger and how it felt tight rather than free and open. I then asked him if he was willing to explore with a trainer if there was any underlying reason for the anger. He was willing to do that.

Ten minutes later he walked back into the seminar room. I stopped whatever I was doing with the whole group and turned my attention to him. When I asked him how he was doing, his whole face lit up with a big warm smile. He let me know that he had felt out of control and had recognized how he wanted to blame me for the emotional discomfort that seemed to come with it.

Immediately there was a mutual understanding, respect and connection between us. I felt inspired by his raw honesty and willingness to inquire what was truly going on for him. The group was inspired by this example of true authenticity and open communication. And a week later he sent me an email:

'What you did with me when I was angry, and more so, who you were during these moments, is something that will probably go with me a long way. You've shown me that strength and vulner-ability can actually dwell together, simultaneously within the same person. When you said that you were actually shaking, I wanted to come up and kiss you, like you would kiss your kid when he's being both brilliant and sensitive. But even then I didn't lose touch with my anger. You did that without depriving me of my anger! So, anger and compassion too can co-exist within us simultaneously. Fascinating! What a rich world is this world of emotions. And you seem to navigate it so nicely.'

These are not the words of a delicate, sensitive, artistic man. These are the words of a strong business coach with a background in the high-tech corporate world. And because they were his, they brought tears to my eyes while reading them.

When 'assumed responsibility' seemed to create pressure and disconnection, a conscious choice was made to explore the illusion of responsibility. It automatically created room for authentic expression of emotional experiences. This simply led to the most inspiring communication between two individuals who had never met before and who subsequently decided to explore the possibilities of working together.

•

Even when control gets dressed up as responsibility, it's still control. Our agreed sense of responsibility is not sustainable. It weighs heavy on our social and professional shoulders, it creates rigidity and ranking and it creates expectations.

Authenticity and passion are great leaders. With them in charge we can lay down the heavy burden of responsibility and allow our interactions in life to become astonishingly inspiring.

Self-inquiry:
Make a list of all the responsibilities you think you have in your personal and professional life. Look at the list and check how it makes you feel... Now imagine your job, your personal life and life in general without any responsibilities. Open the metaphorical doors of your

being, tear down the walls of any comfort zones you are aware of. What do you experience?

COMMUNICATION = INSPIRATION

7. Communication

The fluent dynamics of *leadingship* rely on inspiration. When we experience the passionate expression of authentic qualities we get inspired and decide to follow that lead. Inspiration is therefore dependent on interaction. The most frequently used synonym to interaction is 'communication'.

No *leadingship* without inspiration, no inspiration without communication. This is why the third part of the book is dedicated to it.

•

Everyone communicates and everyone has a unique way of communicating. Because of the differences in our communication we can misunderstand each other. Reality points out how misunderstanding is part of our daily professional and private lives. In fact, it seems to be the perfect condition for economic, political, religious and social conflict.

In leadership context some form of understanding seems to be essential for anyone to follow anyone's lead. As leaders we therefore turn to the communication training programs and studies that are on offer. We learn about delivery and rapport building, about how to polish the content of our message and fine-tune our intention. In itself there's nothing wrong with that. As a matter of fact, I coach and train professionals in this area and I love it.

The question is: do we want to learn communication tools to allow more of our authentic selves to be expressed or to make others follow our lead? What is our true intention?

In my experience a lot of the old and existing leadership dynamics heavily depend on communication skills and techniques to make people do what we want. I call it 'communicational control'. Communicational control seems to be widely practiced in our professional environments. And because it has control in it, it can't be truly sustainable. It can't be supportive of the effortless, inspirational dynamics of leading and following. It's been the main reason for me to explore communicational control and its alternatives.

Through my training programs, coaching and seminars I've come across the widespread assumption that learning more communication skills and techniques will make us better communicators and more influential leaders. Unfortunately it also reflects the belief that our authentic self is not inspiring enough, that it's not good enough to lead. In my training programs and coaching I therefore take time with people to look at communicational control. These people uncover the comfort zone in their communication and explore what happens when they decide to step outside of it. They are invited to try out raw communication without an agenda, intention, rehearsed message or practiced set of skills.

Until this moment I've been awed by the outcome. Trained professional speakers suddenly drop the expert façade and communicate without the layers of veneer. Professionals who used to shy away from expressing their leadership skills take the stage and captivate the audience. Sometimes no words are needed and instant rapport is established. At other times, boundless words of truth find their way out.

The repeated experience in my work made me a believer of 'stripping off the paint and wallpaper' and letting the authentic beauty to be exposed – unpolished, untrained. It only requires recognizing the established comfort zone in our communication and deciding to explore beyond its boundaries. Once the illusion of that comfort zone is smashed to pieces, there seems to be instant understanding and inspiration: the perfect climate for a very sound leadership dynamic.

It starts with saying goodbye to our attachment to communication techniques, strategies and skills. That in itself is hugely powerful and inspiring. To show you how far this simple decision to let go of communicational control can reach, I'll share my experience in cross-cultural leadership dynamics.

Self-inquiry:
In what ways have you ever masked, manipulated or colored your communication to get what you want – privately or professionally?...
How have you used communicational techniques to make people believe, understand or follow you?...

•

I have worked in many different countries around the world with cultures and languages that I previously had no reference to. From the Estonians to the Orthodox Jewish community in Israel, from the First Nations people in Canada to the Zulu's and Afrikaners in South Africa, from the Japanese to the Aboriginals in Australia. In our society we seem to attach a lot of meaning to our verbal communication. I therefore decided to invest in learning at least a few native words and sentences to start a communication built on trust and willingness. Before any seminar or training program I would also get a briefing on the culture, history and communication do's and don'ts of the country I was working in.

It would settle my conscious mind, which was telling me that I didn't know how to connect with these people. And it seemed to work to a certain extend. I also noticed that it cost me energy to keep the acquired information in the back of my mind waiting to be used when appropriate. Luckily I was taught how these little tricks of the cross-cultural trade didn't have to be the main focus of my communication. There was an alternative available.

In 2008 I was asked to go to Canada to event manage a personal growth seminar and then to present another. Apparently 90% of the group of about 110 people would be First Nations people. Even though I was already blessed with a few friendships within that culture, I was told how the upcoming events would be a very different kettle of fish. I would most probably experience a lot of emotionally shutdown and resistant delegates. These people wouldn't trust a white man on stage. They didn't neces-sarily speak or understand a lot of English. And a substantial percentage of them would be subsidized to attend the workshop and would therefore not be present out of free will.

Even though I had been the seminar presenter many times and knew pretty much what was involved in running such a seminar, this was my first time in the role of event manager. And I was thrown into the deep with people whom I could hardly under-stand and who supposedly weren't going to acknowledge me as 'their leader'. Of course my mind was telling me to get out while I still could; it was filled with fear-driven thoughts. So I decided to take some time for myself to invite and fully experience all the energy of thoughts and fear. They came and, because I didn't resist them, they went. Then the stillness gave rise to a new thought: 'What if I don't know and just ask? What would happen if I'd acknowledge the expected leadership position I'm put in, admit that I don't understand their culture and language and simply ask for their help in me supporting them?'

I was tested in the pre-event trainers meeting. The group of trainers consisted of 80% First Nations people. They were quietly waiting for me to tell them what to do, resigning to the fact that this white man was in charge. Without using any of my communication and presentation skills I shared my previous thoughts uncensored.

It was very interesting to see what happened. Even before I had finished two Caucasian trainers started giving me input on how things work in the First Nations culture, what I should or shouldn't do and say. The First Nations people kept their mouth shut, crossed their arms and leaned back in their chairs. So I named what I experienced: the instant resistance among the First Nations trainers and the formularized, rigid concepts and ideas among the Caucasian trainers. I wondered if there was an even simpler option, a way in which the perfect environment could be created for true communication between the different cultures.

A moment of silence... And then the First Nations trainers started speaking. With few words they shared how they appreciated the vulnerability that was exposed, the asking for help and the way in which there was willingness to drop any notions of who they were as a people. They expressed how in general their people valued listening; if we were willing to listen rather than tell, then communication was easy. And they shared that there were no rules of conduct. The only guideline was: if the heart wants to speak, speak, if it wants to be still, be still.'

There was an immediate connection, understanding and trust. No tricks were needed, no skills were used, few words were spoken. The team of trainers became a dream team that was defined by mutual inspiration. A fluent dynamic of leading and following arose. It allowed the use of all individual qualities to be maximized. And it had its effect on the event. From the minute the first delegate registered to the moment I got off stage four days later I didn't experience any resistance, distrust or misunderstanding. I was able to support people in their deepest personal growth work while quite a few of them were speaking in their native tongue; in our connection the understanding lay beyond the words.

One female trainer summarized it very well at the end of the seminar. She shared how she had been raised to hate white people because of all the ways they oppressed the native people throughout history. Experiencing how I opened up the communication to a sense of equality without having to be the same, made her realize something profound: for the very first time in her forty years old life she had not seen native and white people but just people. It was as if skin color and historic background had faded away.

Cross-cultural leadership got a very different meaning to me. Since that time I have experienced instant pre-verbal connection throughout all the cultures I have worked in. It continues to teach me how there seems to be nothing to study or learn for true communication and inspiration. The simple exposure of authenticity and the willingness to drop any notion of expertise seems to be bridging communication gaps that have fuelled misunderstanding and even discrimination for centuries.

And... I still like to learn about cultural backgrounds, language and etiquettes. Why wouldn't I? It can only contribute to our cross-cultural interactions. It most certainly is icing on the cake for any curious human being who wants to dive into a foreign culture. I just realize that it's an indulgence of the conscious mind and that it doesn't define cross-cultural connection, communication, inspiration or leadership.

•

So far it seems that communication skills and techniques aren't the first and foremost condition for effective interaction. Does this imply that we can put our trust in authentic expression no matter what the outcome? Is letting go of expertise and exposing our not-knowing always enough to support healthy *leadingship* dynamics?

My answer – based on my experience to this moment of writing – would be 'no'. The willingness to let go of communicational control and expected outcome seems to be a healthy first choice. To explore the boundaries of any comfort zone in communication, I also look at elements that seem to influence our interaction beyond our conscious choice. To understand what elements I'm referring to, I like to zoom in on the process of communication.

What is communication? Communication is a process of informational input and output. How we perceive information and how we react to it, differs from person to person and from culture to culture. You and I might be in a room that has colored walls and no windows. I might call the walls red and feel trapped, you might call them soft maroon and feel very cozy and sheltered.

The easiest way to explain why our perceptions and reactions are not the same, is through the widely used metaphor of filters. As far as I have experienced we all have filters influencing the way we deal with information coming in and going out. These filters have two jobs: translating any input into something that our internal world relates to and adding censorship to our response. Most of the time we are not consciously aware of their existence. We therefore find ourselves misunderstanding another person and we don't know why.

When one of my associates and I are looking at the balance sheet of our co-owned enterprise our conclusions might be worlds apart. He can see how well we have done in a few areas, while I get concerned about the areas that don't show healthy numbers. His overall verdict is positive, mine is negative. And we were looking at exactly the same numbers. A common phrase used is: 'He is a glass-half-full kind of guy.' And because he is and I appear not to be, we can't seem to understand each other when it comes to our responses. I might want to make cut backs and shut down certain departments while he promotes more investments and branching out. Our intention is the same: maintaining a healthy enterprise. Our different perception and reaction could jeopardize united direction.

Filters make communication prone to failure. Because communication is a requirement for inspiration, it will be very beneficial to look at what filters we have in place. Once we have uncovered what filters can subconsciously influence our well-intended communication, we are no longer oblivious to it. We then have the power to choose consciously whether we'd like to interact beyond those filters or not. People who have chosen to do so have shared how simple it feels. They have expressed how it opens the doors to unbridled, passionate expression of their authentic selves and how it has inspired others to do the same.

I've come to understand that these filters know many forms. Not only do they differ from one individual to the other, they also seem to differ moment to moment. Having said this, all filters have some common ground that is worth discussing in relation to *leadingship*. It's also good to keep in mind that the list of filters in this book will be far from complete; it will only be a guide to explore the possible filters in your own interactions.

8. Filters

In my own interactions and in my work with groups and individuals I have come across the following filters: personality types, gender, belief systems and high impact events. I have experienced how they are not separate entities. They seem to be interlinked. Our gender can have a definite effect on what belief systems we adopt into our experience of life. Whatever personality type we seem to live through, it will draw certain events to us that will match that kind of personality type. For the purpose of recognition we will go through them one by one.

The first filter we will look at is personality type. By personality type I am referring to the archetypes that are based on the Enneagram-model. I have worked with this model since 2003 and I've experienced it to be of great benefit when looking at our interactions with life, systems and people. During my training programs and coaching I take time to explore the rich depths of this model. For the purpose of this book I'll limit myself to a taster. Hopefully it will allow you to recognize how these archetypes largely define our communication.

The Enneagram displays nine stereotypical personality types. Even though we all seem to live the characteristics of each type, there seems to be one that has a special 'grip' on us. Each personality type is defined by certain qualities, desires and communication styles. Even though they show up in each gender, simplicity dictates me to refer to 'he', 'him' and 'his'.

The first personality type is called the perfectionist. This person desires perfection within himself and in the world. He is therefore driven by an ongoing need for the right action. He will try to set himself and other people straight, so that we will all be working towards a more perfect world than the one we were born into. Not succeeding in his crusade for perfection means risking the universe's i.e. God's ultimate condemnation at the end of his life. The perfectionist can be blessed with qualities like pure, ethical, just and honest and tainted by qualities like judgmental, serious, ultra-meticulous, inflexible and angry with himself and others. Communication with others is often experienced as preaching, self-righteous and critical.

The caretaker needs to feel loved and is therefore continuously portraying an image that might be loveable – through caretaking and serving. If people don't respond to this image, the caretaker feels the hollow worthlessness that tells him he is not loved. He is caring, knows how to connect emotionally and uplift others, he is generous and seemingly happy with everything that life offers. He can also be experienced as manipulative, overly pleasing, needy, dramatized grateful and even dishonest. In his interaction with others he uses flattery, compliments, flowery vocabulary and any form of communication that might have people connect to him in a positive way.

The achiever has to be seen as successful – at all cost. It means that he will let people know of his recent achievements, will use namedropping and exaggeration and will razzle-dazzle people into the stories of his success. To back it all up he will often use material image (expensive house, car, clothes) to convince you of his well-earned status, even if he can't actually afford it. Not connecting in this way means that he might not experience the respect and approval that he desires. People often see him as egocentric, opportunistic, vain and pretentious. However, he can also be experienced as optimistic, motivational, empowering, energetic and successful.

The tragic romantic's desire is adoration for his uniqueness. He feels that he is different from everyone else, a bit special somehow, and he uses that to lure people into a connection with him. Failing to do so exposes a kind of black unworthiness that is driven by a fear of being normal like everyone else. He therefore dramatizes his experiences and shares his stories of victimhood to life – not necessarily in a very outward and expressive way, but often one on one. He will also let you know that he can sense what is truly going on in a certain situation or organization. Unfortunately he can be accompanied by jealousy, envy, over-sensitivity, sadness and seclusion. On 'good days' he is creative, gentle, sensitive, observational and warm.

The expert needs to create a sense of safety from emotional or physical pain. He does so by gathering factual knowledge in a rather compulsive way. It serves his belief that the more knowledge he has got access to, the bigger the protection against any painful interaction. He is not a social animal and his interactions are often experienced as nerdy, philosophical, clinical and boring because of the overdose of technical facts. In his attempted isolation he can feel mentally superior, greedy, critical, cynical and cold. When he comes out of his shell people enjoy his focus, wisdom, curiosity, discernment and tender kindness.

The doubter just cannot make decisions because he has put all his trust in the conscious mind. He believes that his mind will keep him and everyone else secure and he therefore feeds his mind with as much know-how about life as possible. After all, life is so versatile that there's a high risk of danger, chaos and thus insecurity. But mind's analytical quality infuses doubt: is this the right action or this? And it often keeps this person locked into a certain position. He wants someone to tell him what to do, but doesn't trust the authority. He therefore tries to include everyone in an equal playing field. He is very social, loyal, competent, supportive, courageously honest and practical. But people often

talk of his distance, spiteful anger, rigidity, suspicion, procrasti-
nation, insensitivity and cruelty.

The enthusiast loves new, different, exciting and fun. He can't do
without because it keeps his mind and body occupied. Having to
stop means acknowledging the possible emptiness that is as
much part of life as the fullness; that prospect is too scary. So his
qualities of enthusiastic, energetic, lively, fun, spontaneous and
entertaining are supporting himself and others to keep the spirit
and tempo up. However, it can become narcissistic, restless, too
impulsive or undedicated. Because of his need for uplifting new
experiences he is often emotionally superficial or shallow, only
likes to talk (fast) about fun and good things and keeps repeating
stories that have provided him with an audience before.

The dominator is charismatic, full of warm-hearted energy,
strong, protective, entrepreneurial and clear. He desires to be the
alpha-male in the pack and therefore controls everything and
everyone - to protect the underlying sense of weakness and
vulnerability. It often brings out qualities like dominant,
controlling, aggressive, entitled, revengeful, superior and
bullying: anything to make sure that he can't be held responsible.
He supports this self-protection by commanding, blaming,
exaggerating, loud and know-it-all communication. Even when
evidence shows that his words or actions were wrong, he will try
to buy your loyalty or blow up the situation so that he can get out
or save the day and thus avoid any blame.

The chameleon cannot live without harmony and balance. When
it's disrupted he experiences a threat of physical annihilation.
Anything that feels uncomfortable is therefore avoided or
stopped. That's why he is a good mediator, without open
judgment, patient, soft, easy going and balanced. It's also why he
can be blamed for his lack of commitment, vagueness, gray

existence, resistance to high or commanding energy or ongoing desire for comfort. His communication is largely defined by compromise, diplomacy, saying yes but doing no, a lack of clarity and a false laissez-faire. Because of his fear of disharmony he merges with individuals and groups. It also means that he looses sense of his own wishes, passion and authentic qualities.

Each need or desire determines how we interact with the world. It filters out whatever doesn't serve that desire and uses anything that might support it. The less we recognize our desires the more our interactions seem to reflect the negative qualities of our personality type. We then brush up against someone else's personality type, which can condemn our interaction to misunderstanding, judgment and conflict.

No one seems to be excluded from the desires, qualities and communication styles that come with our personality type. Communication is therefore served best by understanding and compassion for our own and other people's desires and downfalls. It allows judgment to fade away. It also makes space for the positive qualities that can then be utilized to everyone's benefit.

•

A lot of research has been published on the differences between men and women. Here's an excerpt of generally agreed differences:

Women tend to use nearly twice as many words per day as men. Women take about two seconds to express their emotional experience, men take about thirty seconds. Women can multi-task, men seem to be great in focusing on one job at a time. While women have a need to discuss the challenge at hand, men immediately look for a solution. Women prefer sharing and networking, men focus on claiming territory and fighting the competition.

All of this has to affect the way we process the input and the way we respond to it. It can be very useful to assess whether these gender related differences might be undermining our communication. It has been quite surprising to me to find how many conflicts were simply born out of misunderstanding the opposite sex.

Unfortunately our tendency for stereotyping these differences can cause more misunderstanding. Let me explain this. There are nearly 3.5 billion men - each with individual qualities, characteristics and preferences. Can you see the possible problem when we try to pigeonhole 'typical' male behavior and communication?

Our genitals might point out which gender we belong to, but that's as much as we can honestly say about our (professional) lives as men or women. I have worked with men with distinct feminine physical features and quite feminine behavior who had chosen to explore intuitive leadership. Sometimes my assumption that they were gay was right. Other times it absolutely wasn't. I have coached female executives who looked very feminine. When it came to their communication struggles at work, I discovered how they were displaying masculine behavior to create rapport in a very male dominated corporate world.

In other words, knowing and understanding how gender affects our communication, can be very useful – especially when we include any cross-gender possibilities. It could allow much more understanding of each other's communication. It encourages the use of individual qualities no matter what gender they relate to.

I have experienced again and again how it by-passes the sexual tension that still seems to taint a lot of our professional and private cross-gender relationships. It opens the doors for true non-personal *leadingship* dynamics.

•

In every person's life there seems to be a whole undercurrent of limiting beliefs that filters our perceptions and actions.

If my parents have continuously taught me that the world is a bad place and that I can't trust anyone, how big is the chance that I am completely open to a non-personal dynamic of leading and following? I would probably need to know someone and feel safe before I say yes to his or her lead.

When our cultural background tells us that women are not equal to men, will a woman ever see herself worthy enough to take on a leadership role?

If the school system continuously condemns any out-of-the-box behavior, how much of the available authentic creativity will get full expression?

I've talked about the need to be in control, in charge and responsible: these ideas are also part of our belief system.

And have you ever taken a serious look at all the rules that we live and behave by? Immense amounts of rules seem to get passed on from one generation to the next. They tell us what is appropriate and what is not and can therefore interfere with the authentic expression and communication of the individual.

Society tells us what is expected from a good citizen. The laws and regulations to support those expectations create a rigid frame of reference. These kinds of rules become part of our belief system.

Because there are so many different belief systems, any multi-cultural society is confronted with ongoing tension. What might be true for one social group is not true for the other. Our beliefs also seem to create a world in which there is 'us' and 'them'. This is where our conscious mind thrives. Remember how our conscious, analytical mind needs distinction? It can't get much better than a belief system telling us that our difference from other people gives us certain rights or duties. Because of this segregation our minds get the chance to judge and label others. We create comfort zones with sturdy walls that keep 'those kinds of people' outside our frame of reference. We shut the doors to any authentic interaction that crosses the boundaries of our outlined social group.

•

I mentioned high-impact events as one of the filters. What I mean by them is this. Life seems a continuous stream of events. Somehow most of these events come and go without us consciously registering them. I don't necessarily remember every seminar I have facilitated, I don't remember every cup of coffee I've drunk or every decision I have made. Some events get experienced and seem to then leave that field of experience that we might call 'our life'. And there are events in our life that have made such an impact that we can't seem to forget – consciously or subconsciously.

As far as I have experienced in my self-exploration and in working with others, we consciously or subconsciously hold on to high-impact events. I include both positive and negative experiences. The trauma caused by a dying parent when we were young can have an equally high impact as the moment that we finally get our dream job. These moments become part of who we think we are, the identity we start believing in. And they therefore play their part in determining how we view the world and how we respond to it.

In 2009 I was asked to become the European director of a company that provides leadership seminars. I understood why I was approached but experienced a confusion in my body. On one hand there was excitement because of this new challenge, on the other hand there was doubt whether – despite my resume and experience – I was capable enough. Even though I wanted to accept the new position something was telling me 'no'.

I took some time for self-inquiry. I imagined myself in that new position and checked how the body responded. Doubt came up and turned into fear. The fear got joined by anger and at that moment I experienced a flashback to my student days. In 1993 I was invited to an interview for the presidency of the largest, oldest and very traditional student club of The Netherlands that bears resemblance with an environment like Oxford or Cambridge. At 21 years of age I had the opportunity to lead this 'company' with a 3 million guilders yearly turnover, 27 employees, 3000 members, 15 board members, loads of sub-associations and committees and ongoing media exposure.

I could really feel the pressure of the perceived responsibilities linked to this position. It would most certainly mean stepping outside my comfort zone. And there were three interview rounds to survive. Nevertheless I somehow got the sense that this was meant to be 'mine'. My first interview went very well and I made it through to the next round. Confidence got a big boost and I decided to use that positive energy to study for an upcoming civil law exam. While in my room I could hear my housemates in the room next door. Among themselves they discussed whether I had what it takes to become the next president, and the unanimous conclusion was 'no'. My heart sank. People closest to me doubted my capabilities and it felt as if the passionate desire for this next step in life was infected by it.

It accompanied me through the next two interviews. Nevertheless I was able to present innovative ideas in an authentic enough way. And I got chosen. The day that I got the job I was presented to a cheering crowd of about 1500 club members. My housemates were right in front of the stage, singing, cheering, celebrating. But the 'damage' was done. I might have believed in myself. The club members might have believed in me. And even the very impressive interview panel of former presidents might have believed in me. It all didn't matter because my closest friends didn't. There was a broken link between friendship and new professional challenges.

I recognized the relation between that event and my new decision at hand in 2009: friendship and new career steps don't go hand in hand. It was a friend who asked me to take up this new role and I would be working with a lot of my friends in Europe and around the world. It caused the high impact event of the past to bounce back into my present awareness and it was time to say goodbye to it. What couldn't be dealt with back then and what had subconsciously been carried with me through the years was ready to be let go of. Lesson learnt; time for a new experience. The next day I happily accepted the offer.

Once we get confronted with the limiting effect of a high impact event, we can choose to let go of its energy. In a way it's not real anymore, because it was in the past. We might have had a conscious or subconscious attachment to the pain or pleasure in it and therefore dragged it along with us through time. When we recognize that attachment, we can make a different choice. We can choose to let go, to allow life to take this old experience away from our frame of reference.

One of the most highly regarded leaders of our time demonstrated how. After 27 years in prison Nelson Mandela consciously chose to whole-heartedly forgive the people that put him there and violated various human rights against him. He chose to let go of any resentment that was linked to the painful experience. It opened the doors to true compassion and understanding and inspired people from all kinds of religions, skin colors and nationalities.

·

So what to do with all of these filters? It would be great if we could just press 'delete' and start a new dynamic, wouldn't it? The sooner the better; time is money and we live life only once...

Our professional and personal environment seems to know a lot of time pressure. Everything needs to happen now. Because we want people in our organizations and private life to follow our lead immediately, we depend on an effective communication. Unfortunately our individual filters can be in the way of immediate understanding and effective communication. And it seems that we can only address, understand and let go of limiting filters if we take time to stop and turn our focus inside.

So here is a powerful tension: for more effective communication to create faster results we might benefit from slowing down and inquire what filters are blocking the communication...

Self-inquiry:

Go back to a recent time where you had an argument with your partner, friend or colleague. What was the issue?... Now have a look at all possible filters. What were your desires, negative qualities and communication styles coming through, and what did you recognize in the other person?... What words were you saying and hearing internally and what was the underlying belief?... Could there have been a gender related difference in perception or action?... Did this event seem to be a replica of something you experienced before?... How did it make you feel?... If you could turn back time and communicate with this person again, what would you do or say differently?... How does that feel?...

9. Leadership language

In areas like personal development, communication and presentation skills people are made aware of the importance of non-verbal communication. Based on research from the past it is said that only 7 percent of our communication is dependant on our words. 38 Percent would be covered by our tone of voice and 55 percent by our body language.

Having been trained in personal and professional growth & development and in TV and radio presenting, I have taken this on board and really addressed how I am utilizing the 38 and 55 percent. I started teaching people the same numbers, enjoying the palpable awe and surprise every time these numbers were presented. I copy-pasted this concept without even questioning the words that were carrying this message. I actually paid a lot of importance to the 7 percent. This has made me think.

Once I started exploring the ins and outs of *leadingship* I soon realized how much meaning we truly attribute to words. What we say and write seems to be judged a lot when we are in a leadership position – especially on the work floor, where the mind wants to understand who or what is in charge and why. In most professional areas where leadership dynamics play their part, words are used to make people follow.

Take the spoken and written word away and see what happens. Imagine politics without the debates, written policies and laws. Imagine a business world without press releases and conferences spreading the news of the stock markets, strategic cut backs or merges. Imagine having no access to information – online, in newspapers, magazines or memos - and having to make an important decision based on facts and research. And now imagine yourself as a father or mother not encouraging your baby to speak. It doesn't make sense, does it? It goes against what we are used to.

Experience has led me to believe that the verbal part of our communication takes up way more than 7 percent. And it definitely seems to be true in leadership dynamics. As a matter of fact, as leaders we depend heavily on our verbal communication. Do you recognize 'putting up the technical smokescreen'? It's as if controlling the established hierarchical order is served best by using an abundance of professional, highbrow words and sentences. Without it we could be quite vulnerable because we have no way to influence, manipulate or defend our leadership position. Can you feel the control seeping through?

•

I learned about the assumed relevance of verbal language when I was embodying my first 'serious' leadership position at the student club. One of the main demands of this position was clear communication of any decision. The student club, being the breeding ground for the next generation of politicians, diplomats, captains of industry, lawyers and judges, promoted the skill of the spoken word. We prided ourselves in being the best debaters in the country, not needing physical strength to knock down any opponent. Needless to say that my job came with the requirement of articulate public speech. It was expected that my speeches and debates were traditional in their set-up and vocabulary, that they were laden with intellect and highly entertaining.

Because of my position my words seemed to get weighed very seriously, so I experienced the ongoing pressure of living up to the expectations. However, sometimes the words wanted to come out without any censorship or compliance to the tradition of intellectualized debate. Whenever I had the courage to give in to this urge, the words seemed to touch people. Whenever I suppressed it and tried to manufacture something that would meet the expectations, I found myself struggling and talking to a brick wall.

It created a 'catch-22' situation. I tried to please the people that had elected me and thus let my speech be controlled by tradition and expectation. But by doing so I was not always authentic in my expression, which then prevented the inspirational speech that people were expecting from me. It became one of the biggest personal challenges of that year. The conditioned 'catch-22' only got dissolved many years later.

It's 2010 and after ten years of no visits to the student club I decided to accept an invitation for a dinner with fifteen other former presidents. I was very curious to see how the other presidents, ranging from about twenty-two to seventy years of age, would respond to me. Most of them were aware that despite my substantial resume, despite the available old-boys network and despite the assessments by headhunting agencies I didn't choose to walk the red carpet into politics, reigning law firms or multinational conglomerates. My decision to follow the passion for photography, publishing, travelling and personal growth was not easily understood or accepted by friends and mentors alike. So a part of me that evening was anticipating a gentle inquisition in which I would have to stand my ground verbally.

Luckily the evening turned out to be nothing like that. Sitting at the dinner table I found myself truly enjoying the company of people who share the common ground of having been in the 'hot seat' for a year. Recognizable stories of the olden days accompanied the great food and wine. And then it happened.

Two hundred years of tradition demanded a speech from every individual at the table, starting with the oldest president present. We were treated to amazing vocabulary, superb verbal constructions and witty twists. Each speech received an expectedly good reception – we all realized how we were sharing this evening with 'fellow-masters' of the spoken word.

It was my turn. During the last two speeches my brain had been trying to come up with some content, perhaps some funny anecdote, a surprising start and a funny end, but nothing... I consciously decided to stop the fear-driven spin of compliance and put my trust into the unknown – something I had learned during my first steps of presenting personal growth seminars. Instantly I could feel the passion wanting to come through without me knowing how it would express itself. So I just started talking.

I honestly can't recall much of what was spoken; I only remember how the body felt the energy of the words and how that energy seemed to fill the room. There was a pervasive silence all the way through. And once I was finished I got a roaring 'hear hear'. The rest of the evening was consumed by talking with nearly every single ex-president. Each and everyone shared how they had felt inspired by the words spoken from the heart. They had enjoyed the simplicity and the direct effect it had on them. They wanted to know more about my profession and my passion.

Even though my ego loved getting this recognition I soon realized the non-personal value of this experience. The trust in the authentic qualities allowed the passion to carry the spoken word. It didn't matter if I could construct anything inspirational, entertaining or skilful. Once I stepped out of the way, the words automatically found their way into the hearts of leading professionals who were highly trained in intellectual public speech. By letting go of control, there was space for ease, simplicity and inspiration.

•

I have come across many people in many different cultures and professional environments who seem to share the belief that leadership comes with a certain language. The meaning that gets attached to the spoken word and the form in which it's presented is huge.

It seems to be one of the main reasons for many leaders to start either copy-pasting a version of leadership speech themselves or to find a professional who can train them in leadership communication skills. And before we know it, we hear leaders speak publicly, but we can't seem to really understand them. The trained stereotypical production of words has replaced the authentic expression and falls on deaf ears. It's simply not inspiring.

The question is: what do you choose in this quick sand of verbal do's and don'ts? Communicational control and compliance with the hope for acceptance? Or uncensored speech with the risk of rejection?

How 'should' one speak to co-create any healthy and sustainable *leadingship* dynamic?

•

'Should' is a great example of a word in our daily leadership vocabulary that seems unassuming and harmless. But is it?

We assume that leadership comes with responsibilities. With responsibilities come rules of how to do things; if we don't obey those rules, or if others don't obey the rules, we run the risk of being held accountable. That's when words like 'should', 'must', 'need' or 'have to' come into play. We have grown so used to them that we lost sight of their meaning, application and effect.

When we say 'should', 'must', 'need' or 'have to' we imply that there is no choice – for us or for the people we talk to. And yet everyone has the freedom of choice, always – even in the face of the worst possible consequences of that choice. You might consider breaking the law by doing something you 'shouldn't' and of course it means risking public punishment. Yet, it's still your choice whether you do so or not. You might consider letting go of some of your employees because you run the risk of bankruptcy. There is the choice to fire people or file for bankruptcy; both have their consequences. Even if you are cruelly forced to choose between life and death, you are at choice.

Ask yourself this: does using these words of obligation make you feel light and inspired, do the people you use them towards look and feel enthusiastic? Or do you experience – within you or the team you lead - some urgency, as if in a hurry, being responsible and under pressure?

To this day I haven't come across a single person who genuinely enjoys the feeling of all the should's, must's, need's and have to's that we seem to live and work by. So why would we allow our communication to be colored by them? See what happens when you start deleting them from your action and interaction. If even words are a form of energy, why would we keep using the ones that have a negative load attached to them?

Self-inquiry:
Whenever the words 'should', 'must', 'need' or 'have to' want to be spoken, just stop speaking. Ask yourself what you can replace it with – for example, 'want', 'would like to', 'will', 'am' or 'choose'. And then say the sentence again. Check how this makes you feel different towards the intended action.

•

Regurgitating facts creates know-it-all communication. Know-it-all communication is one of the most common instruments used to establish ranking and authority. 'The more knowledge I display, the stronger my leadership position.' It can cover up any insecurity or vulnerability. Above all it can kill authenticity and innocence, which means that *leadingship* stands no chance.

Instead of exploring the true nature of anything in each given moment, we go along with someone else's version of 'how things work'. We pick up 'facts' in the media, study books or conversations with people who we admire. We then copy-paste them into a next conversation or we form our own opinion on it, which we share with others as being true. And when someone has got knowledge that goes dead against 'yours', you might experience conflict. Do you surrender to his truth or stick to your guns? Who is right? Who needs to listen to whom?

I have been working in the media world long enough to witness how news is not objective at all. An editor has to decide what news will be highlighted. As you might understand, this person has got filters processing input and output. So what makes you think that his choice of news has by-passed his filters? What makes you think that what is communicated on TV, in the newspaper, in magazines and online is objectively true? Even a camera shot is defined by a director's choice. He filters out what he finds important enough to be on the six o'clock news. He therefore says 'no' to a whole lot of events and circumstances that might be just as true – and often much more positively inspirational.

I spoke of copy-pasting facts from study books. It's been quite astounding to me to see what can happen in the academic world. I have experienced how analytical inquiry and academic reasoning outside the box is acceptable as long as it fits a frame of reference that has been created before. Stepping outside the comfort zone of the known can cause a threat to someone's established authority. It also carries the risk of not being understood or accepted. Both of these consequences might persuade us not to explore new truths but to stick to something more acceptable and comfortably known. Yet we base a lot of our 'knowledge' on academic research.

Our society seems to attribute a lot of weight to scientific results published in books, dissertations and newspapers. But the results of any research are highly dependant on filters. Whatever we would like to find determines what we experience and what not. It filters out the elements that might not suit the hypothesis and even hopes. Also, circumstances change because the only constant factor in life is change. So how can there ever be a scientific outcome that is one hundred percent true now and forever? Yet, we refer to science and research as being the only valid and lasting proof to anything.

In my own environment and in my work with people I have noticed how quick we are in telling others 'how it's done' or 'how things work'. However, we don't always have a reference to it from our own direct experience. Maybe our parents have regurgitated this passed-on 'knowledge' and we took it on board as 'true'. Perhaps we have read someone's book that promises us the magic seven steps to inspirational leadership or enlightenment and we decide to believe it.

What was true in one person's experience is not necessarily true in someone else's experience. When you hear someone use words like 'always', 'never', 'I know', 'this is', 'research shows' there is only one thing you can know to be true: it's a reference to the past and therefore it's not necessarily true in this moment.

When you stop the easy copy-paste of 'what is true', when you start exploring the truth of your direct experience, you might find yourself exposed to innocence and the unknown. On one hand this can be a bit scary. On the other hand it takes away the stress of having to proof something and establish your right to a certain position.

Try something different: when someone is asking for your input and your theoretical or empirical knowledge is letting you down, say 'I don't know'. The more you 'know', the more you refer to something from the past. When you drop the notion of having to be knowledgeable, a vacuum of not knowing is created. It could allow space for fresh and innovative input, perhaps not from the chosen leader but from someone else, someone whose passion and qualities are linked to that field of experience. It could allow a neutral maximization of all human resources.

Self-inquiry:
Whenever you hear yourself state something to persuade yourself or someone else, just pause and as yourself: 'Can I know this to be true? Have I experienced this myself or am I repeating someone else's words?' Then ask yourself: 'What is the true intention behind my communication?' If you uncover any form of intended control, of yourself or others, then just stop the communication. How big is the chance that it will actually inspire to increased productivity, loyalty or joy?

•

This is a great time to explore alternatives to the leadership language that humanity has grown used to over time. The illusions of technical smokescreens, verbal dominance and know-it-all communication appear to be non-sustainable. Around the world people seem to stand up to the stream of untruthful communication they have been fed.

We can point our finger at the economic and political leaders, but how have we been guilty of that same untruthful communication? In what ways have you attached yourself to how things should be said or done as a leader? What would happen when you step away from it? When there is nothing holding you back, when you've got full permission to be you, what would you say or not say, when would you speak and when not?

Human beings instinctively pick up which words (or silence) are expressed from authenticity and which from some kind of concept. So why waste energy on manipulating your true expression? Be willing to let go of any preconceived leadership language patterns. You might experience becoming part of a playful and unpredictable communication that lets all qualities rise to the surface when called upon.

Post

At the time of writing, economic 'super powers' are on the verge of bankruptcy. A second global recession in three years time has kicked in. Dictatorial governments are being overthrown. Social unrest is showing up in seemingly stable countries. Influential political, economic and sports leaders are publicly accused of corruption and greediness. The world produces enough food to feed everyone, but nearly one billion people are undernourished. Work-related stress levels are rising in major global economies; millions of working days are lost each year.

If there is a perfect time for a radically new approach to personal and professional leadership dynamics, this could be it.

Throughout history different circumstances have brought forth new leadership concepts. Unfortunately they all seem to have fed the same vertical leadership structure in which an established minority directs the majority. They have offered extra skills, techniques and insights to people in leadership positions. There was the hope that it would infuse lasting inspiration into something that was no longer viable.

It's almost as if we built a dam with the wrong material and keep polyfilling the leaking cracks. Perhaps it is time to let nature run its course.

What would happen if we were brave enough to admit that any preconceived, hierarchical, controlled and structured leadership is past its sell-by-date? What would happen if we valued the qualities of every human being enough to allow the natural dynamics of *leadingship* to emerge?

Chaos? Could be. Once the dam breaks, water will run free and will wash away everything that can't withstand its natural power. If you fear the uncontrollable unknown that comes with stepping outside the old comfort zone, you might be afraid of this temporary state of chaos. But ask yourself this: what is the alternative? Holding onto the so-called 'order' we experience today?

What's the worst that could happen when every single person uncovers the beauty of their own authentic self, when human potential gets utilized to the max, when true communication and understanding ignites countless inspirational dynamics of leading and following, when the real quality of a leadership dynamic is no longer defined by quantity and appearance?

It might mean the end to structures that we have lived and worked by for a long time. And for some this can be a scary prospect too. I've experienced how people fear life and work without structures. I've heard professionals speak of the need for structure because they then 'know' what to expect. But aren't expectations fear-driven projections into the future that create a non-sustainable controlled environment? Life happens, with or without our expectations. Life includes death. Life can take away anything that we expect to be there the next day: health, relationships, jobs, companies, governments, countries, nature...

Some say that human beings need recognizable structure in this three-dimensional world to experience anything. A friend of mine used the metaphor of how the structure of a glass contains the water that we'd like to consume. It made me pause; I took time to digest this plausible input. And then it occurred to me: it all depends on the circumstances. If you want water from the tap and the sink is too small for a glass, you can choose to drink straight from the tap or use your hands. Or: you can stick to the idea of using the glass... you might get very thirsty.

There is nothing wrong with structures as such. The question is: are you willing to face the reality, are you willing to admit that no structure is everlasting?

Letting go of our attachment to existing structures could open up a reality that we haven't been awake to yet.

Just imagine giving up control and saying goodbye to the vertically organized political, economic and social structures of today. Imagine a world of fluent dynamics of leading and following in which flexible collectives of professionals get formed and dissolved according to the needs of the moment, the available individual and collective qualities and intentions.

Wild, isn't it? Perhaps the body is getting signals of excitement and anticipation. Perhaps fear is kicking in. The mind might jump to questions like 'how?' and 'to what result?' Or you could experience how it's quieting down. Whatever the experience, it's worth welcoming it into your awareness. Who knows what will be born from it, how our own perspective on leadership and organizations will change and what innovative input it might provide to even our current social, economic and political structures? At least it will move our awareness away from the stagnant waters of the old and past. It will open the doors to the ever new and fresh life-stream that can inspire to creation beyond our wildest imaginations. Enjoy!

Self-inquiry:
Imagine your personal and professional life being swept away by a Tsunami. No more family, friends, job, organization… just you with the power to choose. It's up to you to create your own life and your only guidance can come from your heart's desires. All your authentic qualities will be available and you can do, be and have whatever your passion tells you to… Where would you go, what would you do, who would you be?

Thank you

All gratitude goes out to life itself, in all its forms and experiences. Life is such an inspirational leader, continuously offering passion-filled opportunities to experience and express the authentic self.

Thank you, thank you, thank you.

What if this was only half of it
— what if your true authentic self
lay in relationship with yourself and
others?

About the author...

Netherlands born ('71) UK resident Arnold Timmerman got his masters in civil and social law in 1997. Instead of pursuing the intended multinational HRM career, he became an editor of glossy lifestyle & travel magazines.

Five years later he turned to his original love - personal growth & development - which has taken him around the world facilitating and presenting seminars to people of all kinds of personal and professional backgrounds, religions, cultures and languages.

In 2009 it was time to integrate this personal growth experience into the professional arena. He became the European director of Conscious Company and started facilitating and presenting leadership seminars in Europe and North America.

Meanwhile, invitations to give leadership clinics, training programs and coaching to organizations and professionals were coming in. These experiences inspired him to launch his own company and to give birth to *Leadingship*.

Arnold's seminars, clinics, training programs and coaching are a reflection of his main interests: exposing the authentic qualities in both individuals and organizations, allowing true passion and inspiration into our personal and professional lives and adding conscious awareness to our communication and to all other dynamics that involve human experience and interaction.

When he is not working Arnold spends quality time with his family, takes to the skies paragliding or enjoys other outdoor activities.

**BUSINESS
BOOKS**

Business Books encapsulates the freshest thinkers and the most
successful practitioners in the areas of marketing, management,
economics, finance and accounting, sustainable and ethical
business, heart business, people management, leadership,
motivation, biographies, business recovery and development
and personal/executive development.